WALKING IN THE
HARZ MOUNTAINS

Quedlinburg - im Finkenherd

WALKING IN THE HARZ MOUNTAINS
Including walks from the Harz Narrow Gauge Railway

Fleur and Colin Speakman

CICERONE PRESS
MILNTHORPE, CUMBRIA

© Fleur and Colin Speakman 1994
ISBN 1 85284 149 4

A catalogue record for this book is available from the British Library.

For our many friends in the Harz.

Advice to Readers

Readers are advised that whilst every effort is taken by the author to ensure the accuracy of this guidebook, changes can occur which may affect the contents. It is advisable to check locally on transport, accommodation, shops etc but even rights-of-way can be altered and, more especially overseas, paths can be eradicated by landslip, forest fires or changes of ownership.

The publisher would welcome notes of any such changes

Maps by Martin Collins

Front cover: The River Oker

FOREWORD

To the best of my knowledge, this is the first time a walking guide for the Harz has been published in a foreign language: here of course in English. I would like to congratulate the authors of this book for the initiative they have shown in undertaking this task. They have taken great care to familiarise themselves with the beautiful mountainous Harz region and have brought together much useful information for the Harz visitor. The eyes of an outsider can often be more objective and see with greater clarity.

Within the framework of the 30 walks described here, a truly representative cross-section of this cultural landscape, influenced by man for at least a thousand years can be experienced; not only wooded mountains and romantic valleys, but in addition the relics of the famous Harz mineral mines, the technical expertise of its water-power in the Upper Harz and the medieval industrial archaeology on the edge of the Harz region. Walking in the Harz can therefore prove an enriching experience both physically and mentally.

For the English tourist there is a special historical connection with the Harz: many English homes in the present century used timber from the conifers of the Upper Harz in their construction, especially immediately after the 2nd World War.

Just as the young woodland has grown and increased since those day, so has the friendship between the peoples of Europe. We hope that this book will be a small addition to this spirit of friendship and will also help the walker to get to know a very special landscape in the heart of Europe.

Dr Albrecht von Kortsflelsch
(Chairman of the Harzklub)

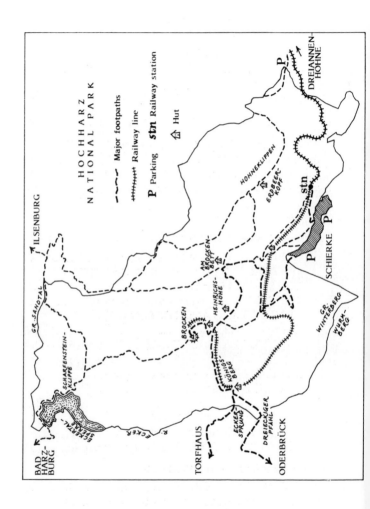

CONTENTS

PART ONE

Before Your Visit

1: WHY GO TO THE HARZ

The Harz Mountains, Germany's most northerly mountainous region, is a paradise for walkers. As rich in natural beauty as in legend, this is one of the most accessible areas in Germany for the walker, easy to reach by road and rail from North Sea ports, served by excellent local public transport, with a choice of accommodation and criss-crossed by superbly waymarked forest and hill paths, to make walking a delight even for the least experienced.

But the region's cultural heritage is equally fascinating. Ancient ore bearing rocks brought Saxon Kings and Princes to seek its fabulous silver, copper, iron and lead, creating towns whose medieval splendour survives. The mining heritage is still to be seen in the landscape but does not dominate or destroy a natural beauty worthy of one of Europe's newest and most distinctive National Parks around the legendary Brocken. There is an extensive Nature Park, countless smaller Nature Reserves, ancient forests and deep gorges where wild boar, deer and wild cats roam.

You'll also find in the Harz, Europe's largest and most extensive narrow gauge steam railway network, a delight for railbuffs and nostalgics alike, providing superb, car-free access to some of the area's finest walking country.

Until 1989 this was a divided land, part of a divided state and a divided Europe. The Iron Curtain ran through the very heart of the region, turning much of the most spectacular countryside into forbidden territory for West and East Germans alike. The East Harz remains a region emerging from a time warp, with old farms and unspoiled villages awakening to the realities of the market economy, and the once forbidden border areas a haven of natural beauty and wildlife of European importance.

2: THE HARZ AS A REGION

Geology and Climate

The Harz Mountains are a vast, oval-shaped range of hills which rise up to 1,100 metres above sea level - around 3,500 feet - out of the Central-North German plain. These hills are not a mountain range in the usually understood sense of the world but what Germans describe as *Mittelgebirge*, a series of massive, largely forested upland ridges which seem higher than their measured height, rising as they do from the low lying areas to the north and east. The Brocken, at 1,124 metres above sea level, is the highest point in northern Germany.

Geologically the Harz can be divided into three distinctive areas. To the west in the former West German State of Niedersachsen (Lower Saxony) is the Oberharz (Upper Harz), dominated by the high plateau around Clausthal-Zellerfeld and cut through with deep valleys. The Mittelharz or Central Harz which straddled the former West-East German border lies mainly in two states, Niedersachsen and Sachsen-Anhalt, with a small section in Thuringen, and is dominated by the great granite massif of the Brocken including the Acker-Bruchberg hills and the high plateau round St Andreasberg. To the east is the Unterharz, the Lower Harz, less dramatic hills consisting of ancient palaeozoic slates and greywacke rock but containing some of the most unspoilt areas of countryside.

The Harz forms part of the Variskian Mountains or Variskischen Gebirge which, thanks to vast convulsions of the earth's crust in Carboniferous times over 250 million years ago, were uplifted above the surrounding plain. As a result of tectonic movements over millenia, ancient underlying palaeozoic sedimentary rocks were forced upwards, eroded, compressed and folded forming a complex mixture of greywacke, slate, quartz and limestone.

There had also been a good deal of volcanic activity, especially in the Oberharz area. Lava and magma which bubbled to the surface led to the formation of the various mineral ores of lead, silver, zinc and copper ore of the mid-Devonian period. The upper Devonian period was the era when iron ores were formed.

During the main period of uplift in the upper Carboniferous

period, huge granite blocks were forced upwards between the already solid and folded rockbeds. The largest part of this granite massif forms the Brocken itself. A pattern of prehistoric flooding, glaciation, and erosion helped to mould the many Klippen or granite tors with their strange weathered shapes, a particular characteristic of the Mittelharz. Ice age glaciers carved deep valleys between the high ranges and smoothed hills.

The climate in the Harz is notoriously ferocious. The Brocken suffers a high rainfall of between 1,500 and 1,700mm per annum, and its steep sides are buffeted by high winds. The west and south-western slopes receive the highest rainfall whilst the east and north-east experience the effect of the drier Föhn wind. The summits of the Harz often seem like islands floating above a sea of mist during winter and autumn.

The Brocken is also known for a remarkable form of temperature inversion when the chilled air sinks into the valleys and plains and causes the temperature to rise on the Brocken summit. The high plateaux attract a far higher degree of sunshine as opposed to the plains, sometimes up to four times as much. The high rainfall encourages the growth of acid heath and peat-rich moorland which acts like a vast natural reservoir for water. Thus the Harz is the source for numerous rivers such as the Bode, Ecker, Radau, Oker, Söse, Sieber and Oder. Its complex system of man-made reservoirs in the valleys is linked by aqueducts which carry drinking water to cities as far away as Bremen and Halle.

The Unterharz in the east has a milder climate and gentler landscape. Its 600-metre high summits are cut through by rivers such as the Bode and the Selke whose deep valleys make up a richly varied landscape. The rivers end in the Saale, a tributary of the Elbe. To the east the hills merge at a height of around 300 metres into the Harz foreland and are bordered in the north by the fertile plain of the Goldener Aue and the Kyffhäusergebirge.

Natural History

The Harz is essentially a forest landscape. Forests are extremely important to the German landscape, covering about 30% of the land mass, and around 80% of the Harz. It's hardly surprising that the Forest - der Wald - features so largely in German consciousness and folklore, nor that modern Germans are so concerned about threats to their native woodlands from pollution and other causes, the much debated *Waldsterben*.

Ancient forests, coniferous on the higher slopes, deciduous in the valleys, once entirely covered the mountain areas. But much of the original forest was coppiced or cut down and replanted in historic times as a result of charcoal burning and the demands for forestry and mining, thus changing the nature of the woodland. In the National Park area, plans are to allow the forest to return to its ancient state as much as possible, and to interfere as little as possible with the processes of Nature.

But in the Harz region as a whole, commercial forestry remains a major land-use, though German practice is to leave areas of semi-natural woodlands and broad, open walks in the forests to attract wildlife and for hunting. The tall wooden shooting platforms - Jagdkanzerl - are a notable feature of the forests, but a love of hunting also goes with a concern for game and wildlife conservation.

Pine, fir and varieties of spruce now dominate the Oberharz and Mittleharz, though extensive beech woods are to be found on the lower slopes. In the Unterharz in particular there are some superb ancient oak, beech and birch woods to add variety to the forest landscape. The deciduous woods are particularly beautiful in spring and autumn with rich colours, and attract considerable wildlife.

For centuries the Harz forests were a source of game with the bear, lynx and wolf acting as the chief predators against the red deer, roe deer and other smaller mammals. The last lynx was shot in 1818 in Lautenthal, the bear and wolf having been exterminated in previous centuries; red deer in particular have increased apace causing much damage to trees and saplings by grazing the bark. Hunting and more formal culling is therefore essential to maintain an ecological balance.

Another characteristic species (best given a wide berth if encountered in the forest) is wild boar. Herds of moufflon, a species of large semi-wild sheep, are to be seen, and the marten and pine marten, the occasional badger, foxes and even wild cats roam freely. More unexpected is the possible sighting of racoon introduced from America and probably escaped from captivity to become thoroughly adapted to the central Harz, noted nest robbers of eggs. Another less controversial re-introduction has been the elegant capercaille, a turkey sized bird only known in the UK in Scotland.

The Harz has a rich flora - both on the high moorland (see below for the Brocken) and around the fringes, in forest clearings and through the ancient, herb-rich meadows in the Unterharz. The tall purple foxglove standing in stately groups even in the centre of dense woodland is omnipresent in the Harz, and is only one of the numerous plants first exploited by Harz people for their medicinal qualities, in this case digitalis as a way of treating heart disease. Arnica, woodruff, and golden saxifrage used against diseases of the spleen are some of the other common medicinal plants. The purple monk's head was used to dye cloth in earlier periods and a number of plants are still used to brew strong herby drinks considered highly beneficial for the digestion.

Anemones, lungwort, lilies of the valley, round-headed rampion and the stag's horn club moss, yellow loosestrife and chickweed wintergreen carpet the ground, while the limestone plays host to such plants as the daphne, snowdrops and lords and ladies with their vivid poisonous red berries. In the meadows are wild pansies, orchids, trollius, poppies, dianthus, cranesbill, toadflax and hawksweed among the more common species to give a blaze of colour to the open fields. Lack of pesticides means that the Harz is a splendid area for butterflies and moths - varieties of fritillaries, red admirals, large coppers and peacocks as well as vividly coloured dragonflies. You'll also see the kind of reptiles increasingly rare in intensively farmed Britain - grass snakes, slow worms and varieties of lizard.

Edible forest fruits abound in the summer - wild strawberries, raspberries, blackberries and bilberries. The woods also contain many varieties of fungi, both edible and poisonous.

The Harz is justifiably famous for its bird life, including the larger birds of prey such as various species of owl, the red kite, buzzard and falcon. Amongst common birds to be seen are blackbirds, dippers, kingfishers, robins, starlings, nuthatches, treecreepers, crossbills, cuckoos, wagtails, and a wide variety of finches, including bullfinches and greenfinches - reflecting the famous story of Saxony's King Henry III who was out hunting finches in the Harz when he was offered the crown in Quedlinburg.

Jays and varieties of woodpeckers are particularly common in the woods.

Human Settlement

Archaeological finds such as prehistoric stone graves point to a pattern of early settlement in the Harz. It was thought that the early settlers came especially from the western Baltic and from central Europe, regions which are now today's Austria and Hungary. Evidence of weaponry and jewellery suggests how Germanic tribes came to the Harz from the north during the Bronze Age, while at the same time the early Celtic peoples also expanded their settlements. The Thuringians, another Germanic people, followed the Celts and pushed into the southern Harz while the Cherusker and later the Saxons thrust the earlier tribes out. By the time of the early Middle Ages as Christianity developed, the Bishops of Hildesheim christianized the population in the hills. Further colonisation continued apace with the discovery of rich veins of silver around 970 on the Rammelsberg hill near Goslar and also lead, copper, zinc, iron and other minerals which began to be exploited in the later Middle Ages.

The mineral wealth of the Harz encouraged the Saxon kings to build their forts and castles close by to defend and exploit that wealth and in the eleventh century Henry III chose Goslar as his residence. Embittered fighting over a lengthy period between the two ruling families of the Guelfs and Staufen was to split the area into small principalities owing allegiance to the states of Braunschweig (Brunswick), Hannover and Prussia.

Mining in the Harz

Mining in the Harz goes back to prehistoric times. Recent archeological finds have established that the smelting of ores was already taking place in settlements around Badenhausen and Düna in the third century BC.

The history of mining in the Harz, however, really began over a thousand years ago in the Rammelsberg near Goslar under King Otto I. Rich silver deposits from this mine soon filled the imperial treasure chest, producing the coins which financed the regime. Nearby Goslar became the imperial residence for a succession of

Emperors who held court at the Kaiserpfalz. The town of Goslar became a major centre of trading activity, eventually becoming a member of the celebrated Hanseatic League, the influential late medieval north European freetrading organisation. The number of ruined monasteries, castles and fine residences on the slopes of the Harz testify to the region's former economic importance.

Mining activity continued apace throughout the Middle Ages, but then declined after the fourteenth century caused by ravages of the plague and also technical problems, but the sixteenth century, a period of great technical innovation, saw a return to prosperity. Export of Harz silver and other minerals was soon to extend as far afield as England and Russia.

Further technical innovation and mechanisation in the nineteenth century again increased the mine's prosperity, helping to build Germany's industrial might. Even as late as after World War II, the Rammelsberg mine was still able to produce most of West Germany's copper, a third of its silver and more than a quarter of the country's requirements for zinc and lead. Finally closed in 1988, the thousand year old mine has now been converted into a fascinating Museum of Mining, with much of its water-powered system still in place in the old workings.

But the Rammelsberg was only one of scores of mines which were opened throughout the Harz from late medieval times onwards to work the area's vast mineral wealth, and which have left a dramatic mark on the landscape.

Since there was comparatively little settlement in an area where the growth period for cereal crops was all too short, it was initially difficult to attract enough workers to the mining industry, particularly the skilled craftsmen, that were needed to extract and smelt the ores. The various feudal overlords who owned the mines and mineral rights were forced to make certain concessions known as Bergfreiheiten to attract the right quality of skilled men. These rights included freehold to build their houses, timber for building, firewood, tax concessions, exemption from other feudal-style duties and from military service, and the right of individual miners' settlements to hold their own free markets where necessities could be imported duty free. The miners also had brewing rights and grazing of animals in the hunting forests was also allowed. Numerous miners and smelters came to settle in the Harz from the Erzgebirge region in Saxony, and to this day local people have retained a distinctive dialect.

The seven mining towns of Zellerfeld, Clausthal, Wildemann, Lauthental, Altenau, St Andreasberg and Grund were established in the fifteenth and sixteenth centuries, close to the rich mineral veins and became the first industrial towns in Niedersachsen, later banding together as an industrial entity.

In order to smelt the silver, present in galena (lead ore), it had first to be smelted with charcoal so the works became established at such centres as Zorge, Bad Lautenberg, Lerbach and Gittelde.

Mining required vast quantities of timber for props, machinery, buildings, fuel, especially for charcoal. As ancient forests were cleared, quicker growing spruces were planted instead of slower growing deciduous trees while large areas in time became denuded of timber.

Peat was tried experimentally as a substitute fuel by Graf Christian Ernst zu Stolberg-Wernigerode in the eighteenth century, and by 1736 there were six peatworks on the Brocken - the name Torfhaus is a reminder. The problem lay in drying the peat after it was cut and enormous drying houses, five storeys high and fifty metres long, had to be built containing gigantic iron stoves to burn the peat as a substitute for charcoal.

Another landscape feature is the network of mill ponds, dams and channels initially to provide water to help flush out and wash the ores, but also to channel the heavy rainfall and harness waterpower. Complex waterwheel systems were developed to drive the heavy machinery to bring ores to the surface and crush them before smelting.

The Harz was one of Europe's first industrialised areas, active long before the Ruhr. There were about 25,000 inhabitants in the Oberharz alone by the late seventeenth and eighteenth centuries, mainly earning their living from mining and related industries.

By the twentieth century, falling prices for metal and the increasingly high cost of mining caused most of the mines in the Harz to close: St Andreasberg in 1910, Clausthal-Zellerfeld in 1930 and the Rammelsberg in 1988. The only working mine open today in the West Harz is called the "Hilfe Gottes" at Bad Grund, and though ores are still imported from other parts of the world for processing, the recession of the early 1990s has seen further contraction of the industry.

Mining has also left a permanent mark on the landscape, not only old workings and former spoil heaps, in most cases already relandscaped or renatured and overgrown. Many of the former ponds, dams and leets have become carp ponds or attractive lakes for a variety of recreational purposes, especially sailing, boating and swimming.

In the late twentieth century, tourism along with forestry has become the Harz's most important industry, with many of the former mining settlements now being transformed into attractive inland resorts, offering an excellent choice of accommodation and related facilities. The area is particularly renowned for winter sports, being Germany's first recognised ski region, whilst a network of waymarked cross-county skiing routes crosses the region. In the summer months the Harz is justifiably celebrated for its outstanding opportunities for serious walking with everything on offer from substantial cross country hikes for the more experienced to easy waymarked strolls from car parks.

3: THE BROCKEN

The 1,124-metre high Brocken occupies a very special place in the German imagination. For one thing it is the highests mountain in northern Germany; its dome-like summit crowned by towers and masts make a distinctive landmark over a considerable distance.

It is also the focal point of countless legends and folktales which have attracted and fascinated many celebrated writers and notabilities such as Johann Wolfgang von Goethe, Heinrich Heine, and Hans Christian Anderson over the years.

One of the earliest written accounts of the Brocken was in 1575 by one Johannes Tal, who published an account of the Harz flora after a Brocken ascent, this being Germany's first example of such localised botany. Gottfried Oleabius climbed the Brocken in 1656 and said that the fantastic shapes of its rocks and tors seemed like innumerable tables for witches to dance on. Not surprisingly the appropriate crags soon came to be known as the Hexenaltar,

Hexenwaschbecken and Teufelskanzel - the Witches' Altar, Witches' Washbasin and Devil's Pulpit.

The Brocken's connection with witchcraft was largely a seventeenth-century literary invention which emerged at a time when anti-witch frenzy was waning and harmless tales taking their place.

Goethe (1749-1832) climbed the Brocken in the winter of 1777, a season when it was a particularly dangerous and difficult undertaking, unheard of at that time of year. After first being refused, he was finally able to persuade forester Johann Christoph Degen to guide him up the mountain. As the pair reached the summit the mists parted and the sun shone down on them from the heights.

The little summit shelter or Wolkenhäuschen (little cloud-house) now bearing a Goethe plaque was constructed in 1736 by the Count of Stolberg-Wernigerode, as a stream of Brocken visitors began to make their way up the mountain and were often overtaken by bad weather. This little shelter was extremely basic and was only meant as an emergency measure. A guest house had been built by the Count in 1743 with a sort of summerhouse, but Goethe was to find the accommodation closed on his memorable climb.

Goethe writes in retrospect after his visit to the Brocken of the amazing colours on the Brocken "... the most gorgeous purple colour appeared, then its shadow became green, then changed into sea-green or it could be called emerald green so great was its beauty..."

The devil and the witches supposedly hold their rites on the eve of May 1st, Walpurgisnacht. Fascinated by the legends, Goethe returned to the Brocken in 1783 and 1784 and made two additional visits to the Harz area. He used the mountain as the setting for the rites of Walpurgisnacht in his epic drama *Faust*, giving literary sanction to the rites alleged to have taken place on the summit when local witches celebrated the end of winter and the coming of Spring.

Many other writers, artists, botanists, aristocrats and diarists followed in Goethe's footsteps. Among them was poet Heinriche Heine (1797-1856) who declared of the Harz:

> I want to climb the mountains
> Where the dark pines tower upwards,
> The streams roar, the birds sing,
> And the swaggering clouds chase each other.

For Heine the Brocken was the most German of all the mountains, reflecting all his nation's most positive and negative virtues. On the plus side it seems to breathe an understanding, a sense of tranquillity and tolerance because its elevated position allowed it to see so much: "When such a mountain opens its huge eyes, it can probably see a lot further than the dwarfish human species."

Heinrich Heine's *Harzreise*, published in 1826, opens with a famous paragraph on the university city of Göttingen, celebrated for its university and its sausages! He not only describes his route across the Harz, a hazardous climb down a mine shaft, the specialities of the places he passes through, but also the various people he meets, in a delightful ironic vein. His feeling for the landscape has lyrical expression as he describes the mountains:

> Standing as if dressed in their nightshirts, the pine trees shook off sleep from their limbs as the fresh morning wind combed their hanging green hair, the birds were holding their prayer meeting, the Wiesental sparkled as if it was a golden cover sprayed with diamonds and the herdsman strode over the scene with his flocks to the sound of their ringing bells.

His actual route, still known as the Heineweg, descended from the Brocken summit along the present Brockenstraße then through the Ilsetal to Ilsenburg (Walk 13).

In 1800 a Berghaus was built on the summit to provide accommodation. This was burned down a year later and was rebuilt as a hotel. By the mid-nineteenth century the Brocken had become a place of pilgrimage for every literate German who wanted to visit the historic spot where Faust and Mephisto had celebrated Walpurgisnacht. The tourist industry had begun in earnest.

The wonderful effects of light and colour at sunrise and sunset on the Brocken began to prompt demands for an observatory. At certain times the effect of sun and light on the clouds forms a haze which throws gigantic shadows of people on the mountains as if they were spectral figures. In 1838 measurements of wind and weather were being taken with a special thermometer and by 1895 a two storey house was built as an observatory, to be followed by a larger more suitable stone building in 1912. The branch railway from Schierke bringing even more visitors was opened in 1896.

With the coming of the railway, Walpurgisnacht became an annual festivity which was celebrated by chartering a special night train to the Brocken summit. In 1910 for example a festively decorated locomotive with its eleven carriages and 500 passengers dressed as witches, wizards and devils arrived at the gaily decorated Brockenhaus and were addressed by the Mayor of Ebeling who declared that they were here to drive out the winter and welcome in the summer. Further speeches, eating and drinking and jollifications followed, the menu having suitable devilish names.

Hermann Löns coined the slogan "More protection for the Brocken" as the Harz started to be developed as a major tourist area. Even more tourists came after World War I and in 1935 the Reichsnaturgesetz made the Brocken, Acker and Bruchberg and much of the Oberharz a National Nature Reserve. The television mast on the Brocken erected in 1935 led to another world first in 1936, the experimental beaming of the albeit notorious Berlin Olympic Games over a limited area.

The Brocken summit was badly bombed by the Americans in 1945 who mistook it for a V2 base, but it was cleared in 1948 and open to walkers from the East; the border barring those from the West from reaching the summit. Later the Brocken with Schierke and Ilsenburg and other villages became part of a five-kilometre wide no-go area, though some limited access was still allowed till the 1970s. A three-metre high concrete wall round the Brocken and high wire cross-country fences protected by gun towers, searchlights, dogs, border patrols and horrifying tripwire machine guns made the mountain totally forbidden territory for twenty-eight years, with many would-be escapees dying at the hands of the feared Border police. The summit radar stations became the nerve centre of the German Democratic Republic's spy centre with radar and radio systems, linked to Soviet systems, able to listen to conversations as far away as Holland and France. Ironically, the Americans on the nearby Wurmberg summit above Braunlage were also listening to conversations in the East as far as Warsaw.

When the Berlin Wall was finally breached in November 1989, many people in both East and West Germany felt the time had also come to reclaim the Brocken. On 3rd December 1989 barely four weeks after the end of the Wall, thousands of people from the former East and West Germany joined in a great Brocken ramble, the first which had taken place since the 1930s. It was understood that part of the summit would still remain as a forbidden area though sections might be opened up. Many ramblers - many of them from the East, members of the once forbidden Harzklub - carried banners with them demanding that the gate to the actual Brocken summit be opened.

About 12.50pm, quite unexpectedly, a member of the Red Cross Mountain rescue team came out and told the vast crowd now assembled outside the locked gates that the gates would be opened and that there were only ten unarmed frontier guards who would help to organise an orderly stay on the summit. The crowd responded with wild delight and the only proviso was that they must not enter the summit building. Fortunately fine weather made this no hardship. The Brocken ramblers laughed, danced, sang and celebrated. Thus was the Brocken summit, for so long forbidden territory for German people, peacefully retaken, to become a symbol of freedom, peace and reunification, and, as Heine had forseen, truly the most German of mountains.

4: THE NATIONAL PARK HOCHHARZ

Over 100 years ago in 1890 a naturalist and director of Göttingen University Botanic Gardens, Professor Albert Peter, established an Alpine garden on the summit of the Brocken. Its purpose was to research the way Alpine plants were able to adapt to the severe Brocken climate and he was keen to make his garden available to the general public.

Despite the neglect of two World Wars and their aftermath, Professor Peter's Alpine garden has survived. During 1971-1989 when the Brocken summit increasingly became militarised and difficult of access, such Alpine plants as mountain avens, the alpine snowball, the campanula, the melancholy thistle, masterwort and

Alpine sorrel still survived. Also to be seen are healing plants like the great yellow gentian whose roots were used medicinally for digestive disorders or for schnapps and arnica which was used as a tincture to heal wounds.

The Brockengarten, as it is now known, is cared for by the new Hochharz National Park which was founded in September 1990 as one of the last acts of the short-lived democratically elected Government of the former GDR immediately prior to legal unification.

Unlike UK National Parks, which are more akin to the German Nature Parks, National Parks in Germany receive stringent state protection, with nature protection and conservation of wildlife habitats receiving the highest priority. The National Park is just 6,000 hectares in size and consists of the Brocken summit and surrounding areas of high granite moorland and ancient forest area round the Brocken itself.

National Park objectives are to protect the upland areas of the Hochharz, including, its forests, moorland, water courses and fauna and flora. Like all National Parks in Germany the Hochharz is subject to stringent zoning. In the core zone, or Zone I, the most vulnerable area, plants and animal life enjoy maximum protection from human impact and therefore access is limited to a few clearly marked paths. Fallen trees are deliberately left lying so that the natural cycle is interrupted as little as possible and much natural regeneration can take place.

In the intermediate zone of Zone IIa, effort is made to conserve and stabilise the forests, as in the past a good deal of tree and plant cover had been cut down, which, as a result, left remaining trees particularly vulnerable to storm damage and the leaching of nutrients. Re-stocking with native deciduous trees such as beeches from the nearby Elendstal valley are among recent conservation measures.

In the third Zone IIb or outer zone, there is a greater compromise between protecting the environment, public access and making use of some of the timber in the forest. There is an emphasis too on good forestry practice and woodland management.

The National Park contains the largest concentration of natural mountain pines in Middle Germany. Typical of the area too, around

900-1,000 metres above sea level, is a mosaic of small-scale high moorland areas which are white with cotton grass in summer. There is also the subalpine Matten vegetation which is characterised by such species as the Brocken anemone (its tousled withered head is called witch's broomstick) endemic to the mountain, and the Brocken hawkweed. The rocky areas with their distinctive granite Klippen or crags are particularly rich in rare lichens and dwarf shrubs. Species of woodpecker, owl, capercaille, grey wagtail, dipper, and nuthatch are some of the most characteristic birds, whilst larger birds of prey to be seen include buzzard and kite.

Characteristic mammals include the wildcat, wild boar, foxes, roe and red deer. Squirrels and woodmice add to the variety of wild life. In the woods the tall foxglove is omnipresent in forest clearings and on the edges of the woodland. Among 170 varieties of fungi recorded are *fomes fomentarius,* useful in fire-lighting so solid and dense is its make-up, while the moorland blooms with varieties of sundew and heather. Various orchids and arnica brighten the meadows, also skimmed by a cornucopia of colourful butterflies.

One benefit of being a military border zone for four decades has meant that wildlife - plants and animals - could thrive to a degree unknown in more heavily visited or farmed and forested areas.

The concept of the National Park Hochharz is also to protect the Kulturlandschaft or heritage landscape. The National Park looks after sites which have evidence of prehistoric or early cultivation and industrial activity including areas where mining, ore smelting, charcoal burning, peat cutting, glass-making and quarrying have taken place in the past.

Though visitors are always welcome, the National Park is particularly concerned to maintain the balance between the care of a unique, ecologically vulnerable environment and visitor enjoyment so that this highly vulnerable area suffers as little as possible from the impact of mass tourism.

The re-opening of the Brockenbahn steam railway from Schierke in July 1992 proved highly controversial. It was strongly opposed by the National Park Authority, supported by conservationists and naturalists throughout Germany. Environmentalists pointed to the fact that up to five litres of lubricating oil could be spilled into water courses by 1930s designed steam locomotives on each individual journey from Wernigerode and that up to 3,000 extra visitors per day were crowding onto trains to the already over-visited summit with all the new demands for visitor facilities that would bring.

In 1990, the Hochharz National Park Authority inherited an ugly, semi-militarised landscape on the Brocken Summit of radar, wireless and television stations, surrounded by concrete walls and military roads. A small Russian Army barracks remains, residue of the Cold War, soon to vanish into history. Even when they have finally departed, the summit will take years to restore to a semi-natural state.

Whilst most militaria have been removed, sections of fence and a single watch tower remain as a potent symbol of man's inhumanity to man, whilst a surviving radar station has been transformed - ironically - into a temporary museum for National Park information, though still containing mementoes of the terrible Grenzpolizei or border guards. The hotel is being rebuilt and new cafe and sanitation facilities installed.

Faced with the effects of mass tourism, the National Park Authority has undertaken a policy of visitor "canalisation". A former military style road around the summit is being retained and improved with landscaping to allow the thousands of visitors - up to 35,000 per day can arrive on foot or by train - to enjoy the incomparable views without trespassing onto the vulnerable moorland or forest. The Brocken Garten remains open for a short period for guided visits each morning.

Dr Uwe Wegener, Deputy Director of the Hochharz National Park, sees the new National Park as a step towards a united Europe and a unified Germany rather than just a national monument. Included in future plans are a wildlife park, an extension of the Alpine garden and a national park headquarters which will be available as a congress centre as well as a central information point.

Discussions are taking place with interested organisations in the neighbouring Niedersachsen State to create an adjacent National Park in the former West, taking in much of what is now the Oberharz Nature Park in the Oberharz. There are many interested groups to be consulted, but at time of writing it seems that an extended National Park taking in some of the finest scenery of the Oberharz is about to become reality.

The National Park and Nature Park are of course only the

highpoints of an area of magnificent countryside, all of which merit utmost care and protection, not least being the lovely Niederharz whose unspoiled villages and neglected farms form a naturalist's paradise. The Harz is truly a part of our common European heritage.

5: THE HARZKLUB

Es grüne die Tanne
Es wachse das Erz
Gott gebe uns alle
Ein fröhliches Herz

*(The pines clothe themselves in green, the ore grows
underground, God give us all a joyful heart)*

This ancient Harz motto adopted by the Harzklub, one of Germany's oldest and most influential voluntary outdoor and conservation organisations, encapsulates two essentials of the Harz region, its forests and its mineral wealth.

The Harzklub - Harz Club - was founded in 1886 at a time when Germany was developing rapidly politically and economically after its unification under Chancellor Bismarck and in the wake of the Franco-Prussian war of 1871. The rapid rise of industry meant the growth of huge conurbations around towns and cities with often grim living conditions for the masses. Those concerned at the loss of the countryside formed themselves into local and later regional voluntary groups concerned to ensure that there should still be some unspoiled countryside for those who enjoyed walking and natural beauty. This voluntary tradition in conservation and access matters continues to flourish in the present day Federal Republic of Germany as an important part of the democratic process.

In the Harz a few enlightened people such as the Quedlinburg publisher H.C.Huch, railway director Albert Schneider and Captain Robert Spatzier discussed the possibility of a Harz Tourist Association. This was finally formed in Seesen as the Harzklub in 1886 and by the time of the first Annual General meeting in Goslar a year later, no fewer than twenty-three representatives from branch organisations were also present. Significantly, encouraging tourists from North German towns to enjoy their leisure in the mountains was not the Club's only goal, equal weight being given to guarding and protecting the forest and preventing malicious damage.

By the end of the century efforts were being made to develop the Harz for summer visitors, but at the same time attempts were also made to stamp out accommodation profiteers. Footpath routes were marked out and way markings were made uniform. There was continuous concern that preventive measures be taken to avoid damaging the area on account of visitor pressure. In 1889 the first Harzklub walker's map appeared.

In 1899 Otto Schulz said about the threatened Bodetal valley: "Ways and means should be found to carry out important economic projects without causing great devastation, so that the romantic appeal of the Bodetal is not harmed." This form of pragmatic environmentalism has been the hall-mark of the activities of the Harzklub ever since.

Ten years after its inception, the club had 10,000 members with 98 branch organisations and the Harzklub had spent the equivalent of about 15 million DM at today's prices for the encouragement of tourism. By 1909 membership was 19,000, a figure still higher than present levels as the majority of those members were from the east where the Harzklub was banned from 1945.

Already as the century opened the Harzklub was successful against the building of a dam in the lower Bodetal area between Thale and Wendeburg. It was also successful in preventing motorways, funiculars/cable cars in vulnerable moorland areas and in promoting the recultivation of former mine spoil heaps and tips. Care of rarer fauna and flora was undertaken on land either owned or leased by the Club. Even as early as 1909 motor traffic in the area was seen as a growing problem, whilst a special interest was taken in preserving and encouraging vernacular styles of architecture.

The Harzklub actually continued to exist throughout the Hitler era, but its officials were chosen for it. But it was soon banned in Communist East Germany.

After two World Wars, at least in the West, it was seen as more important than ever that the Harz should remain a quiet recreation area, particularly for those who were working in the conurbations to the north and west of the Harz. This led to a successful campaign for the establishment of the Naturpark Harz - the Harz Nature Park - covering more than 80,000 hectares of the finest countryside in the Oberharz, the western part of the Harz mountains.

However, this proved to be little protection against the building boom in the prosperous 1970s which unleashed an array of totally inappropriate and rather ugly building in many Harz towns, causing the then chairman of the Harzklub, Hermann Kerl, to coin the phrase "Manhattan in Harz". This set off a renewed consciousness and concern for the environment and architectural style which was soon to take effect on the planning authorities. Buildings began to be modified and more sympathetic styles adopted, whilst industrial remains and spoil tips were renatured.

In 1980 the Harzklub celebrated the twentieth anniversary of the Harz Nature Park. The present chairman Dr Albrecht von Kortzfleisch has, among other things, given the Naturpark Harz a new up-to-date symbol and has been particularly concerned to promote the Club's work through the new walkers' maps and as editor of the Harz journal *Unser Harz*. As Dr Rolf Denecke says so presciently in the journal's special anniversary issue in 1986, "boundaries are never absolute and have frequently changed even in peacetime and especially in Central Europe".

As soon as the boundaries between former West and East Germany were opened, an avalanche of visitors from east and west poured into the Harz to discover what had so long been denied them. The Wanderheime or walkers' hostels in Torfhaus and Sonnenberg were full to bursting with the new arrivals. The older members of the Harzklub from the East brought out their old flags and banners from secret hiding places. After the successful storming of the Brocken on Sunday 3rd December 1989 there was widespread jubilation. On 3rd October 1990, less than a year later, the new

Chairman of the Ilsenburg branch of the Harzklub led the singing of the Lutheran hymn "Now thank we all our God" in front of the Wolkenhäuschen on the summit of the Brocken.

The first eastern Harzklub branch group was reformed in December 1989 and many other areas quickly followed suit. A great deal of work was set in motion by members the Harzklub. Old routes between East and West were reinstated, now no longer divided by deadly mines, watch towers and fences, and many paths were newly signposted and new, accurate maps for the whole Harz were produced for the first time for decades. By the 1990 AGM in Bad Lauterberg, there were already thirty-three newly founded or re-formed East Harzklub groups.

The Harzklub now has over 16,000 members and operates about 2,600 public guided walks annually with about 50,000 walkers taking part. Many walks also cater for specialist interests. The Harzklub produces its own maps in partnership with the State Survey Offices as well as waymarking each of the routes with distinctive symbols. The club also has four hostels for overnight accommodation and members enjoy discount on the cost of their stay. As well as caring for paths, information boards and waymarkings, it looks after footbridges, benches, shelter huts, viewing towers, barbecue areas, nature trails and other public facilities including refreshment facilities, small museums, industrial archaeology and natural features and monuments. It collects its own Harz archive and documents on Harz dialect and local skills. The wearing of traditional Harz costume and the encouragement and practice of local customs and dances (like the charming Grasetanz danced by women and young girls) add to the enjoyment and understanding of Harz culture. Individual branches also organise activities for children and youth groups.

The Harzklub also promotes its ideas by means of the written and spoken word, school competitions, guided walks and media activity. The club is able to act as an advisor to the Harz Nature Park and also to the new Hochharz National Park, especially on footpath and access matters, a prime example of close voluntary and statutory authority co-operation and partnership so typical of German countryside management.

The Harzklub's address is: 38678 Clausthal-Zellerfeld, Bahnhofstraße 5a, Germany, Tel: 05 323-81758

Train arriving at Hasselfelde

6: THE HARZ NARROW GAUGE RAILWAY NETWORK

The 131km gauge railway network through the Harz mountains is Europe's finest narrow gauge steam railway.

More than a mere tourist attraction or a historic relic of the steam age, this railway forms a vital all-the-year round transport service through the region. Its survival owes not a little to the accidents of history, not least to the old East German regime which placed its preservation as a working technological monument higher than the achievement of profit. Until recently it was also a busy freight railway and whilst freight has declined catastrophically with the collapse of the old GDR smokestack industrial base, its new role as one of the region's major tourist attractions poses new opportunities and new challenges.

The railway was built in stages, at a time in the later nineteenth century when narrow gauge railways were seen to be a cost effective and logical solution to the technical problems of building railways through difficult mountainous terrain. Though plans to have a railway across the Harz mountains mainly to carry timber and minerals to link in with the standard gauge railways at Nordhausen

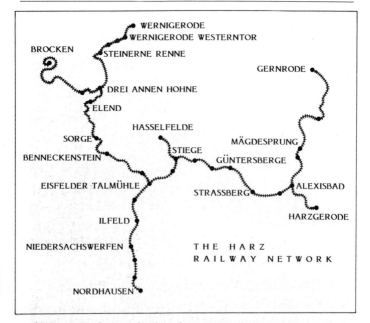

and Wernigerode went back as far as 1869, the first line actually to be built was the Gernrode-Harzgerode Eisenbahn or Selketal line between Gernrode and the ironworks at Mägdesprung, which opened in 1887. By 1892 this had reached Hasselfelde, with a spur to the little mining town of Harzgerode.

By 1896 another company, the Nordhausen-Wernigerode Eisenbahngesellschaft had been formed to build the main line route, and work started from both ends on a project which now included a link to the 1,142 metre high Brocken summit. This was reached and the railway to the Brocken opened in October 1898, a major feat of engineering, and the network through to Nordhausen completed by 1899. The final 13.5km stage to link the two railway networks between Eisfelder Talmühle and Stiege was completed in 1905, the final part of a remarkable railway which survives more or less intact to date, complete with charming period stations preserved by half a century's benign neglect.

Two trains leaving Alexisbad, Selketal

The building of the Harz railway was a considerable engineering achievement and experienced engineers and workers from Italy, Yugoslavia and Bavaria were called in to assist with track laying, the building of 400 bridges and viaducts, one tunnel, level crossings and considerable water drainage works. A good deal of blasting through rock was also necessary. The trickiest terrain was the Brockenmoor itself from where 90,000m^2 of earth had to be moved to make a firm foundation for the track bed.

Significantly enough, the railway company's logo was the yellow canary - the Harzer Roller - used in the Harz mines in former times as a means of warning miners about poor air quality; if the birds stopped singing this was an effective early warning that something was wrong.

This is no mountain rack railway, but a metre gauge line depending purely on adhesion, where the track serpentines its way through narrow valleys and around the mountainside to ensure that the maximum ruling gradient was no more than 1 in 25 - still steep enough for even a powerful 2-10-2 steam locomotive hauling well laden coaches, and with curves as tight as 60 metres.

For decades the Harz Railway - known as the Harzquerbahn and nicknamed the "Quirl" after the noisy way it shook and careered through the forest - was a lifeline for the region, carrying tonnes of timber, minerals, stone, iron, chemicals and raw supply for local industry. Lack of private enterprise competition in former East Germany allowed it to remain the principal freight carrier in the region. It was a local railway linking villages with towns, and also a busy tourist line, beloved by walkers, specially the Brocken branch which during the pre-war years reopened each season on Walpurgisnacht (April 30th) as the snows melted, with specially decorated trains crowded with revellers determined to celebrate magic and mystery on the mountain top.

The two railway companies were taken over by the nationalised railway undertaking Deutsche Reichsbahn in 1949 and incorporated into the national rail network. Whereas in former West Germany, decisions were taken in the 1960s to close the narrow gauge lines from Braunlage, in the east, with lower car ownership, railways still mattered. In 1955 came a historic decision to replace the ailing fleet

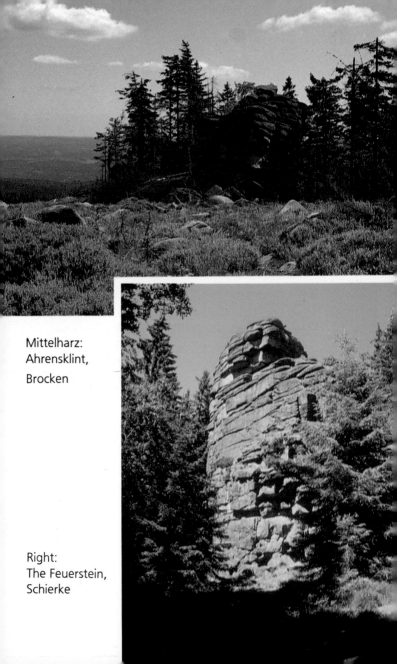

Mittelharz:
Ahrensklint,
Brocken

Right:
The Feuerstein,
Schierke

of vintage steam locomotives with a brand new fleet of modern steam locomotives, based on a pioneering example built in 1939. These powerful 700 horse power 2-10-2 tank locomotives, seventeen of which were built at the Karl Marx works in Potsdam between 1954 and 1956, still provide the mainstay of motive power on the line.

It is this fleet of engines, supplemented by a few "old timers" dating back to 1897 (which are used for special services), and some less than popular diesel locomotives which operate the daily train services. There are also two delightful little "Triebwagen" or single coach diesel railcars. Rolling stock are traditional carriages with old-time open balconies which are a joy to travel on, and a superb way of enjoying the scenery and wild life of the Harz at a civilised pace through the heart of the forest.

In 1961 at the height of the Cold War, the Brocken became part of a five kilometre "Sperrgebiet" or forbidden zone. Services to the Brocken summit were suspended and special permits had to be obtained even for GDR citizens to visit friends or relatives in border villages on the Harzquerbahn such as Sorge, Eland or Schierke.

In 1990, after the Berlin Wall came down and the two Germanies were united, there followed a long and fiercely contested debate about the future of the Harz railway which was now losing huge amounts of money. Though most people wanted to see the line retained, reopening the Brocken branch proved highly controversial. On the one side rail enthusiasts and local tourist industry foresaw huge international interest in a steam railway to the summit of central Germany's highest mountain; on the other conservationists, naturalists and the newly established Hochharz National Park saw all the problems of pollution and congestion this might bring, with each train bringing up to 500 extra people to the mountain's already crowded summit.

The issue reached cabinet level in the Land (State) Parliament, with environmentalists finally losing the battle and in April 1991 a decision to reopen the Brockenbahn was taken. After a symbolic special service in October 1991, the regular service was reinstated from July 1992, the restoration and rebuilding having cost some 20 million marks. However agreement was reached to operate no more than five return trips a day, and not to run winter trips.

Single 1930s diesel railcar near Mägdesprüng

The debate continues, but there is hope that the compromise will be to develop the railway network as part of an environmentally friendly public transport network for the region, reducing dependency on private cars, and in doing so, much reducing the congestion and pollution caused by tourist traffic. Moreover, by using local trains and buses you are actively helping the local community in the Harz. Income from tourist traffic helps to sustain the local public transport network which otherwise could not survive. This benefits the local economy, helping to keep jobs in the area.

But as well as being environmentally less damaging than car usage, the Harzquerbahn and its branches - now being privatised into the Harz Railway Company - and linking buses offer far greater flexibility and interest in planning a variety of walks than the inevitable circular walks to and from a parked car. Why take a car if such excellent public transport exists?

It is to take advantage of some of the many superb opportunities for exploring the Harz mountains on foot, by train and linking bus, but especially using the unique Harz narrow gauge railway network itself, that this book has been written. In our view this is what is truly meant by sustainable tourism.

7: GETTING AROUND THE HARZ

You can get to the Harz mountains from the UK and elsewhere in Europe by a variety of means - by car from the Channel ports along the motorway system via Hannover and Hildesheim to the Northern Harz, by Kassel and Göttingen for the South Harz. If you're flying, Hannover has the most convenient airport; it also has the best Inter-City rail links from Holland and the Channel ports and also from the Channel Tunnel.

From Hannover's main station, the Hauptbahnhof, direct trains go to Goslar and Bad Harzburg around the northern edge of the Harz from where there are connecting buses to such centres as Wernigerode, Braunlage, St Andreasberg and Clausthal-Zellerfeld. The southern Harz can also be reached from Hannover via Northeim, from where a direct train service goes to Herzberg (branch line to Bad Luterberg), Bad Sachsa and Walkenried to Nordhausen, with links to Stolberg or via the Harzquerbahn to Schierke and the Selketalbahn - though the last rail connections of the day are relatively early, which is a problem if you are arriving at either Nordhausen or Wernigerode in the late afternoon.

Public transport within the Harz is extremely good. In the west Harz, several north-south bus services, some of them former narrow gauge rail services replaced by bus, operate to common timetables in the regional rail timetable. These services penetrate the area, not only making it easy to reach most of the main population centres and tourist areas by integrated road and rail services, but provide excellent internal services for a variety of route planning.

Most of the walks in this book make use of that integrated transport network and for this reason it is worth acquiring local rail and bus timetables, available at bus and rail stations throughout the region. Cook's European Rail Timetable available in the UK from Cook's Travel Agents and some bookshops contains most of the local rail services in the Harz including the Harzquerbahn and the Selketalbahn.

Do remember, however, that if you are planning to alight at one of the many unstaffed halts on the Harzquerbahn and Selketalbahn railways, (marked with an X next to the station name on the timetable) you must inform the guard of your intention, otherwise the trains will not stop. In order for them to stop, you need to ensure that the driver has time to see your clear hand-signal well before the train arrives at the appropriate point by the platform.

The pocket-sized DB Regionalfahrplan for Braunschweig, Harz and Göttingen costs just 5DM and is an excellent comprehensive bus and rail timetable for the Oberharz and much of the Mittleharz area south of Goslar and Bad Harzburg. These are available from DB stations in the region or in advance from DB offices in Germany.

The equivalent pocket timetable for Sachsen-Anhalt does not include bus information. There are two main (privatised) local bus companies operating in the East Harz. KVG Wernigerode, who operate from Wernigerode as far as Thale and Nordhausen and Magdeburg, produce an excellent, comprehensive bus and rail timetable available from the Wernigerode Tourist Office (2DM) or direct from KVG Wernigerode, Dornbergsweg 5-7, D-38855 Wernigerode, Germany (tel 09433 36 33 1).

The Quedlinburg, Harzgerode, Selketal, Stolberg and East Harz area services are operated by Transport und Reise GmbH Ballenstedt, Hoymer Straße 21, D-4303 Ballenstedt, Germany, who are a somewhat more old fashioned outfit but with a useful network of services to supplement the rail network. They have an office just to the left-hand side (as you leave) of Quedlinburg Station.

Basic information about German rail services, rail passes and copies of the Kursbuch and regional timetables can be obtained from any staffed rail station in Germany, or (from the UK) from German Rail, Suite 118 Hudson's Place, Victoria, London SW1V 1JL.

Tickets and reservations from the UK to Germany and within are also available from BR International, Victoria Station, London SW1 (tel 071 834 2345).

DBAG's (Deutsche Bahn Aktien Gesellschaft) own travel agency, DER Travel Service of 18 Conduit Street, London W1 offer a range of travel ticket and rail-based package holidays in Germany.

A number of independent international rail appointed travel agencies in the UK also handle DB tickets. Ultima Travel of 424 Chester Road, Little Sutton, South Wirral, L66 3RB (tel 051 347 1717), have a particular interest and specialist knowledge of the German rail system and have offered to provide a comprehensive and bespoke booking and reservation service for readers of *Walking in the Harz Mountains,* including Inter-Rail, German Rail Passes, Regional Rail Rovers and Eurotrain tickets, and insurance services designed to meet the needs of rail travellers. When contacting Ultima, please mention this guide.

Russell Hafter Holidays of 26 The Square, Ashfield, Dunblane, Scotland, FK15 0JN (tel 0786 824515) is the only UK travel firm specialising exclusively in walking holidays in Germany. The firm offers a number of attractive self guided walking packages specifically in the Harz Mountains, including packages based at Alexisbad and Drei Annen Hohne, both excellent centres for many walks in this book. Walking maps of the Harz can also be supplied. Most Hafter holidays also offer luggage carrying facilities. Again mention this guide when contacting the company.

8: FOOD AND ACCOMMODATION

Although there are perhaps fewer regional specialities in the Harz than in some other areas of Germany, food in cafes or serviced accommodation is almost always of a high standard and usually attractively presented.

Frühstück or Breakfast is normally served buffet style except in smaller hotels and guest houses and there is usually a choice of fruit juice or perhaps fresh fruit or fruit compote, crisp rolls and rye bread. Jams and preserves are frequently home-made and there is an excellent range of local honey. A variety of cheeses including the famous Harzer Käse, oval shaped and cold meats plus boiled eggs (usually soft boiled) complete the usual fare. Tea or coffee are equally popular, so if you prefer tea to the excellent coffee, do remember that continental blends are weaker than English blends and taste better with lemon or "Schwarz" (without milk or lemon), though you can of course take milk if you wish.

Snacks are usually available any hour of the day, but mid-morning or late afternoon is the traditional time to taste the really excellent cakes available in most Konditorei or confectioners with the drink of your choice. Wine, beer, tea, coffee, mineral water and a variety of soft drinks including the usual proprietary brands are available everywhere. A particular refreshing combination is Mineralwasser and Apfelsaft (mineral water and non-alcoholic apple juice) known in most regions as Apfelschorle. Savoury snacks are traditionally either a couple of Frankfurter sausages with some bread and mustard, or alternatively freshly made Thuringer Bratwurst, tasting best of all grilled over charcoal, or a cheese and bread roll.

Beer is almost synonymous with Germany as the old Reinheitsgebot or Purity Laws of 1516 lays down strict guidelines on its manufacture. As well as the usual national names, there are several excellent local brews in the Harz with distinctive flavours - look out for Gils Brau brewed in an open plan brewery in the centre of Goslar, Harzquelle from Halberstadt, Einbecker from Einbeck where they invented the first strong "Bock" beer, and Haßelroder with its distinctive capercaille logo from Haßelrode near Wernigerode. The Harz is not a wine growing area, but wines from the Rhine, Mosel and Baden area and occasionally from Saxony are always available. Among schnapps and herby spirits to be found in the Harz are such regional specialities as Norhäuser Doppelkorn, a powerful schnapps and Schierke Feuerstein, a strong, herby drink invented by a local chemist and now a popular aperitif.

Mittagessen or lunch still tends to be the main meal for many Germans and if you're eating out, the Tageskarte or Table d'hote at two or three courses is usually very good value for money in most restaurants. This is usually soup (either a stock-based clear soup, Goulaschsuppe or perhaps a vegetable soup) followed by a tasty meat or fish dish with salad or vegetables and maybe a sweet course such as ice-cream. The latter garnished with fresh Harz bilberries is a typical and delicious Harz dish. Fresh asparagus in season is a famous speciality and another typical Harz dish is Grünkohl with Schmorwurst, very tasty and consisting of kale (skilfully prepared), sausage and boiled potatoes. The Harz is also noted for its excellent game dishes including venison, wild boar, or hare and there are also very good trout. Chicken and duck are also widely available. For Abendessen or the evening meal, a similar range and variety of food is on offer. Vegetarians may find life a little more difficult except in more sophisticated towns such as Goslar which has one or two vegetarian restaurants. Abendessen can again be either a snack or a full meal with a similar bill of fare to Mittagessen, though some Harz families sit down to Abendbrot in the evening: largely a mixture of cold meats and cheese to which you generally help yourself.

Prices of food in Germany are generally similar to the UK, despite the high value of the Deutschmark, and quality is extremely high with an emphasis on natural products and purity. On the other hand if you are self catering or organising your own packed lunch, supermarkets in every town or even village will offer an excellent choice of fresh bread, fruit and cold meats for prices which compare well with the UK. Prices of certain commodities in the former East Germany are notably cheaper.

Given the Harz's long tradition of hospitality, there's no problem over choice of accommodation from the simplest bunkhouse or youth hostel, to typical medium priced Gasthofs (always excellent value for money in Germany), small hotels and luxury hotels. Private accommodation or farmhouse accommodation can again be highly recommended for anyone on a modest budget, and again offers an opportunity to meet local people and share their way of life - a good principle of responsible tourism. You'll generally find an excellent choice of self-catering accommodation, cottages or apartments, available. There are also numerous facilities for camping either with tents and caravans or motorised caravans.

Our advice is to book your accommodation in advance in the high season especially in the popular areas, which includes much of the former East Germany, but accommodation can usually be found even at busy times if you're prepared to take the risk and to look around. Remember in Germany the main school summer holidays are staggered from early July right through to September, and September is also an extremely popular month for late holidays in walking and mountain areas.

The first point of contact for accommodation is the Harz Tourist Office, Harzer Verkehrsverband e.V, Marktstraße 45 (Gildehaus) D-38640 Goslar, Germany (tel 49 (0) 5321 3404-0, fax 49 (0) 5321 3404-66). Literature is produced in English as well as German, and the introductory guide gives a detailed breakdown of all other tourist offices throughout the region; a letter to the relevant local office will give you accommodation lists by return with a huge range of accommodation in almost every town and village in the Harz which can be booked direct from the UK by letter or phone usually at prices which even with the relatively high German mark, will seem notably less expensive than equivalent accommodation in the UK.

Youth hostel accommodation in the land which invented youth hostels is plentiful, and is detailed in the International Youth Hostel Federation Handbook. Though you can get a guest pass for an occasional night in a German hostel, it's far better to be a member of your own national Youth Hostels Association (UK addresses: YHA England & Wales, Trevelyan House, 8 St Stephens Hill, St Albans, Herts AL1 2DY or Scottish YHA, 7 Glebe Crescent, Stirling FK8 2JA) with an International YHA card and access to the IYHF Handbook. There are also hostels run by various German outdoor and walking organisations including the Harz Club.

Health and medical care is excellent in Germany on both sides of the former Border. UK travellers should have the form E111 with them just in case a visit to a local doctor is necessary to entitle them to free treatment in any EEC country. In some cases payment for certain services or medical supplies may have to be made, but this can usually be reclaimed through your own DHSS office under reciprocal arrangements. Full medical and personal insurance when you are travelling is, however, essential for any holiday or extended visit.

Whilst you'll probably be able to get around the West Harz without difficulty just speaking English - young people in particular tend to be very fluent - it can be a little more of a problem in the former East where until very recently Russian was the second language. But everywhere if you do have some German, even just a few basic words and phrases, it'll add enormously to the enjoyment and pleasure, even when mistakes are made, and help to make contact both with local people and with fellow walkers.

9: ACCESS, FOOTPATHS AND MAPS IN THE HARZ

In common with the whole of Germany, the Harz region enjoys full Betretungsrecht - the walker's right to roam - throughout its forest and mountain areas, but in practice this access is restricted both in official nature reserves and in the "Kern zones" of the Hochharz National Park. The Harz Club however, strongly request their members and friends to keep to the excellent network of official waymarked paths, as a way of minimising damage to delicate eco-systems and to wildlife habitats. It's also common sense to do so in densely forested regions without obvious landmarks where the risk of getting lost is fairly high.

Waymarking of footpaths in the Harz is excellent. However, it is important to understand the system and how it works.

Because of generous public access rights, Germany does not have a system of Definitive Rights of Way as in the UK. In theory at least all tracks and paths shown on a map are open. Waymarked routes are categorised in terms of their function, the waymarking largely being undertaken by voluntary outdoor and walking organisations. In the Harz mountains, this body is the Harzklub, through its network of local groups throughout the region.

The highest category of footpath routes in the Harz are Long Distance Routes (Fernwanderwege) and Major (Hauptwanderwege) routes. These are indicated by a continuous red line on most footpath maps.

There are four important long distance routes across the Harz mountains. Two of these are international routes - European Long Distance Footpath E6 represented by a white St Andrews cross on a black ground, which runs between the Baltic Coast and the Adriatic, crossing the Harz from Goslar, Okertal, Altenau, to Bad Harzburg in the south, and the Netherlands-Harz Long Distance Route, also represented by a white cross on a black ground but also with a letter N. This route crosses Lower Saxony from Holland and then along the northern edge of the Harz from Seesen through Wolfshagen, Goslar, Bad Harzburg, Ilsenburg, Wernigerode, Blankenburg to Thale.

Two other important routes feeding into the Harz are the Hildersheim-Harz route - marked with an H on a black ground, and the Solling-Harz, marked with a white S on a black ground.

The Hauptwanderwege on the other hand are all purely within the Harz region. There are six such routes - three through the West Harz, three through East Harz. The three in the West are Hauptwanderweg 1 (waymarked with a red spot) running from Seesen via Lautenhal, Hahenklee, Torfhaus, Eckersprungen to the Brocken; Hauptwanderweg 2 (green spot) from Goslar to

Schulenberg, Altenau, Steiglitzecke, and Osterode and Hauptwanderweg 3 (blue spot) - the Kaiserweg (Emperor's Way) which runs from Bad Harzburg to Molkenhaus, Olderbruck, Braunlage and Walkenried.

The three in the east are as follows: a route (blue spot) from Bad Harzburg along the Niederlande-Harz route to Thale then to Ballenstedt, Harzgerode, then down to Stolberg and Nordhausen. Second is a blue St Andrews cross route from Nordhausen to Wernigerode via Trautenstein, Königshütte, Elbingerode and Wernigerode. Third is the blue diamond route from Schierke to Thale via Elend, Königshütte, Rübeland to Altenbrak and Thale.

All are superb routes and extremely well waymarked. Because they require more than a day to complete, they are outside the scope of this book, though sections of them are used in individual recommended walks.

The second grade of routes in the Harz are what are known as Zielwege or Destination Routes - point to point walks, usually linking towns and villages and with them public transport nodes. These are shown with dashed lines on the maps, and, in the West Harz, with an accompanying numbering system which makes it easy to identify your chosen routes at a crossroads or intersection.

The third and lowest category of routes are short circular walks for motorists, Rundwanderwege, which start and finish at car parks. These are waymarked with a coloured triangle within a circle - the number of the individual walk is contained within the triangle. Colour coding represents the likely time required to complete a route: blue routes last about an hour, yellow two hours, red three hours.

Rundwanderwege are shown on the Harzclub maps as a red dotted line. Full details of all the circular walks in the West Harz are contained in the booklet *Wegweiser Naturpark Harz: ein Wanderführer* by Günter Auberg and Dieter Frey, published by Bayerische Verlagsanstalt, Bamberg.

Route destinations and distances are indicated at crossing points on a tree or free-standing signpost by the characteristic Harz Club metal shield signs with the fir tree logo. White wooden boards, rimmed with red with a Harz Club symbol are also common. Each route with its appropriate symbol (and number) is given together with distances to the nearest kilometre.

In between main crossing points, the waymark symbol is used as a painted symbol or metal disc along the route on an appropriate point, usually a tree, generally at a point where a decision on direction has to be taken, but sometimes just as reassurance. The important point to realise is that the symbol used is often that of the highest category of path along that particular stretch of path or track, rather than having a plethora of symbols. So if the path you happen to be following runs part of its way along E6 international long distance trail, the red triangle of your route may be subsumed under the white cross of the higher category on a black ground, until the routes separate, and then you're back with your red triangle again.

It sounds complex and over formal, but once understood it makes route finding, which otherwise would be a nightmare through a thickly forested landscape like the Harz, relatively easy. Having said that, it is important to check waymarks carefully, as a missed waymark can result in real difficulties once you lose a path - though if that happens, the area is so thickly served by paths, it is only a matter of a few minutes in most cases before you rejoin another waymarked route onto your original way.

Most walks in this book take advantage of either Hauptwanderwege (main routes) or Zielwanderwege, the point to point walks. The high quality of waymarking of these routes makes it possible to keep route description to a minimum, to give more information about what is to be seen on the way, and more walks in the book. Nevertheless, we cannot emphasise enough the need to use this book as no more than a supplement to good quality, up-to-date maps.

Maps and waymarks used together are the only way to get around the Harz. This book is not intended in any way to avoid the need for good map reading, though we hope it will add to the pleasure of discovering some super walks.

Maps

There's a bewildering variety of good walking maps available for the Harz region. The ones we recommend are the 1:50,000 series produced by the Niedersächsisches Landsverwaltungsamt

Landesvermessung (NLL) - the nearest equivalent to the UK Ordnance Survey, though without any National Grid Reference system indicated. These maps, in their bright blue covers entitled *Naturpark Harz* covering an area from Seesen, Osterode and Herberg to the Brocken, and the newer *Wandern im Mittleren Harz* are both the official maps of the Harz Club, and contain up-to-date details of waymarked footpaths using the official waymarked symbols, and, in the West Harz, numbering system. In common with many German walking maps, the NLL series have excellent detailed information printed on the reverse which if you read German, gives you useful summaries of the area's geology, natural and local history. But even if you've little or no German, maps have a universal language which, linked to the appropriate waymarked symbol, make them easy to read.

Another useful and widely available map at the same scale which covers a larger area including the whole of the Selketal, with maps printed on both sides of the sheet (but with less topographical information), is the olive coloured *KV-Plan Auto + Wanderkarte* of the entire Harz. This also shows the official Harz Club waymarked routes with both symbols and numbers (make sure you get the latest edition - the fourth came out in 1993 and a fifth may be due soon), and also an introduction by the Club's Director.

Other maps currently available include the popular bright green Kompass series, sheet 798 covering the West Harz, a handy size with good topographical and tourist information on the reverse. From our experience, whilst these are good maps, the detail of paths is less clear, nor is the Harz Club's numbering system used. The Kümmerly + Frey Tourist Verlag map offers clearer maps with excellent detail, but use of greens and yellows for waymarked paths blends disconcertingly into forest or can be confused with minor roads.

Sadly, there is nothing we have discovered in Germany to compare with the detail and accuracy of the UK Ordnance Survey Pathfinder or Outdoor Leisure series, amongst the best of their kind in Europe. Some useful maps of parts of the Harz do exist at the larger 1:25,000 scale, but in general they appear to be blow-ups of the 1:50,000 base maps and though easier to read do not necessarily give more information or greater detail. The *Regiocart Wanderkarte*

(RV Verlag) of the Oberharz is a case in point, the details of Winterskiing routes actually making purely walking information more difficult to read. You'll also find special local maps at 1:25,000 scales around specific resorts such as Goslar, Wernigerode or St Andreasberg. Such maps usually have detailed town plans on the reverse, and good local information, and for that reason are therefore worth buying if you're staying in a particular location.

Our advice for most purposes, however, is to keep to the NLL series or the KV map, but also to buy the latest editions when you arrive - supplies available in England (Stanfords, 27a Floral Street, London, WC2 9LP. The Map Shop, 15 High Street, Upton-on-Severn, Worcs. WR8 OHJ. Tel: 0684 593146 keep a variety of maps of northern Germany) are likely to be a year or two old when you buy them, fine for advance planning but unlike Britain which has a definitive map, waymarked routes are often altered for a variety of reasons, for example building development, or forestry, upgrading for vehicular traffic, or even wear and tear or perhaps by a diversion away from an increasingly busy tarmac lane onto a quiet footpath as traffic has increased. An up-to-date map will contain the latest information, though inevitably there are occasions when the waymarking has been changed before a new edition of the map has been produced. Our advice in such circumstances is always to follow the waymarks.

Mittelharz forest pony

PART TWO
The Walks

THE OBERHARZ (Upper Harz)
Walks 1-10

The Oberharz consists of the area of the West Harz in the Harz Naturpark in Niedersachsen: a region of high, thickly forested ridges cut through with deep, narrow valleys such as the Oker and the Oder, and several reservoirs. There are more than 3,000 kilometres of waymarked footpaths through the Naturpark alone.

The best centres for exploring the Oberharz are undoubtedly Goslar (a magnificent medieval town with excellent public transport links to the entire area) followed by Bad Harzburg which also has an excellent choice of accommodation and a good railhead with buses both to Braunlage and Wernigerode; other good centres include Altenau, Clausthal-Zellerfeld, Braunlage and St Andreasberg in the central areas, and Bad Lauterberg, Herzberg, Osterode and Bad Grund in the south.

WALK 1: OKERTAL
Oker Waldhaus to Altenau

The narrow, rocky gorge of the lower Okertal provides a romantic introduction to this spectacular valley, dominated by huge reservoirs, en route to the forest resort of Altenau.

Distance:	15km (9¹/₂ miles)
Time:	5 hours (some climbing)
Public transport:	Bus 2432 from outside Goslar or Oker Railway Station to Waldhaus and return from Altenau (approximately two hourly); the walk can be terminated from inter-mediate points along the bus route.
Parking:	Waldhaus 2km south of Oker on the B498 Altenau road. Return by bus to Waldhaus from Altenau.
Map:	Naturpark Harz 1:50,000
Refreshment facilities:	Waldhaus, Romkerhalle, Altenau

Route description: Take the track from the car park and bus stop at Wanderhalle (red triangle and white St Andrews cross waymark - E8 6F) which runs alongside the River Oker, soon entering a deep, rocky gorge of the Okertal. Keep on the main E8 route, the path now climbing to become a scenic walkway past pine hung crags above the river, with handrails for safety. The path passes the first of a series of small dams and hydro-electric works; at Adler Klippen (Eagle Crags) there is a fine viewpoint looking upstream.

The path descends to the river. Cross the bridge to the road, turning right, continuing along a narrow path between crash barriers for 500m before taking the path back to the riverside and crossing the bridge below the reservoir wall of the Lower Reservoir. Continue on the wooded path past the little artificial lake, then along the river, past Celler Insel back to the far side of the valley. The path now follows a lovely area of open riverside, and continues through woods before emerging at Romkerhalle. Cross the footbridge past the Gasthof to the main road to see the waterfall.

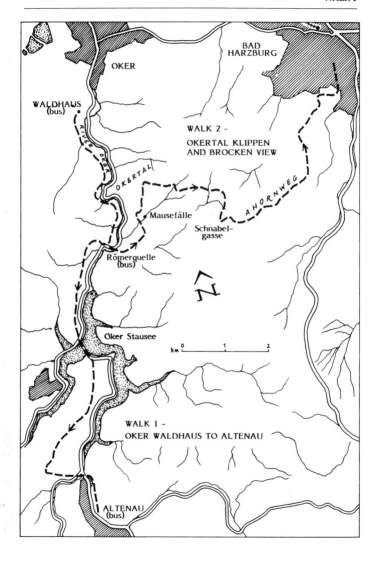

The route continues left along the main road through the narrow gorge for around 300 metres before ascending to the right (E8, also blue triangle) into Großer Birkental. Keep left at a junction of paths, along the side of the hill with the great Okerstausee - Oker reservoir - ahead. Immediately past the road over the bridge, bear left, still with E8 white cross on black, descending steeply to the main road. Cross the bridge, following signs to Altenau (E8, blue triangle; paths 6D, 7P) climbing up a steep hillside and following a long thickly forested ridge south-westwards, Dietrichsberg, for around 3km until waymarks and signs direct you sharply to the right downhill into the outskirts of the resort of Altenau. Turn right along the main street into the town centre; buses return approximately every two hours to Waldhaus or direct to Goslar.

Points of interest:

Okertal: This spectacular valley with its romantic crags and rushing river lies at the centre of what is known in the Harz as the "classic square mile of geology" with ancient granites, slates, volcanic rocks and Devonian limestones compressed into a small area. The Okerstausee - the Oker reservoir - contains 47.5 million cubic metres of water and is typical of many reservoirs created in the Oberharz valleys to provide water for surrounding conurbations as well as hyrdro electric power. There is free access around its shores.

Romkerhalle: Once in the ownership of a countess who claimed the inn at Romkerhalle to be an independent kingdom, it now boasts a themed restaurant with exhibitions of heraldic devices: a good place for a coffee stop. The 50-m high waterfall falling down the sheer cliff face opposite the restaurant makes a dramatic feature.

Altenau: Altenau, now a moorland and forest resort lying at the crossroads of many cross-Harz walking routes, was the youngest of the seven Oberharz mining towns which in the seventeenth century formed themselves into an industrial group noted for their production of silver and iron ores. Many of the houses are of typical Harz clapboard mining architecture. There is also an attractive seventeenth-century wooden church.

The Bruchberg just to the south-east of the town is, at 928m, one of the highest peaks of the Harz.

WALK 2: OKERTAL KLIPPEN AND BROCKEN VIEW
Romkerhalle (Okertal) to Bad Harzburg

This walk linking the Okertal and Bad Harzburg takes in a number of spectacular weather worn Harz Klippen or Tors, followed by forest tracks with fine views.

Distance:	12km (7 miles)
Time:	4 hours
Public transport:	Bus 2432 from Goslar or Oker Station to Okertal-Romkerhalle; return from Bad Harzburg (train or bus)
Parking:	Park at or near Oker Station and catch the 2432 bus, returning to Oker Station by train or bus.
Map:	Naturpark Harz 1:50,000. Route map p49
Refreshment facilities:	Romkerhalle, Kästeklippe, Bad Harzburg

Route description: Alight from the bus at the Romkerhalle. Cross the road to where the footpath 23B (yellow spot), signed Kästeklippe, leaves down a narrow side valley formed by the Romker stream.

This path soon begins to climb steeply. Keep to the yellow spot waymark at a junction, the path climbing sharply up a ridge through dense forest. As it emerges there are fine views across to a series of granite crags or tors (Klippen) that protrude above the forest.

The path climbs up to the first of these - the Feigenbaumsklippe, the fig tree tor, so called because of its fantastic shape. Steps and safety rails take you to a little viewpoint platform with a magnificent outlook across the surrounding hills and forest.

Retrace your steps to a path along the ridge past more extraordinary formations - the Mausefälle (mousetrap), the Hexenküche, (witches' kitchen) and the Kästeklippe, the latter at 606m a fine viewpoint on the highest point of this remarkable ridge. Close by is an inn, and buses link Bad Harzburg from the nearby track and road junction.

Summit of the Mausefälle near Okertal

Turn right at the next junction, still with the yellow spot and signs for Bad Harzburg, along 6L or 32B. The track curves around the hillside for the next 1¹/₂km; at the next junction keep with the yellow spot, the track continuing to contour around the hillside before emerging at another junction by a small walker's shelter.

Turn right, due south here, this time with a yellow triangle (170) signed for Torfhaus. Keep along this route for about 2km as it ascends a steep and narrow ravine known as Schnabelgaße - literally the beak alleyway on account of its narrowness - at the side of the Brietenberg hill. This climbs to a crossroads where a red triangle route joins from the left.

Turn sharp left here, but after a few metres go right at the next junction down the route with the blue triangle, 17P known as Ahorn Weg or Mapletree Way.

This is a lovely open track, the forest thinning out to give fine open views. From several points along here there are superb views of the Brocken, including points where the trees have been felled in long firebreaks or avenues, known as Brockenschneise, above a narrow stream, the Riefenbach.

The Ahornweg follows the contours of the hillside before curving northwards to meet the main path to Bad Harzburg through a lovely area of beechwoods, over a hill known as the Papenberg. The path swings round the edge of the hill to join a steep lane which descends into the town centre, with a choice of cafes and inns.

Bad Harzburg railway station and main bus station is at the north end of the town's long main street.

Points of interest:

Romkerhalle: see Walk 1
Harz Klippen: These fantastic, wind and frost carved granite tors or crags on hill tops or along ridges are a typical feature of the Harz mountains. As in other parts of the world, they are often given names to denote their fantastic shape frequently, as in some of these examples, linked to Witch or Devil legends.
Bad Harzburg: see Walk 3.

∗   ∗   ∗

WALK 3: THE ECKERTAL
Bad Harzburg circular

Distance:	15km (9$^{1}/_{2}$ miles)
Time:	4$^{1}/_{2}$ hours
Public transport:	Train or bus to Bad Harzburg; take a local town bus out to the Wolfsklippen at Sophienhöhe on the eastern edge of the town; otherwise it's an additional 2km walk from the station due east along Julius Straße, under the motorway and along the main Ilsenburger Straße. Route 50D (blue spot) does however utilise quieter roads to the north via Abendröder Straße and Eichendorf Straße.
Parking:	Bad Harzburg
Map:	Naturpark Harz 1:50,000
Refreshment facilities:	Bad Harzburg, Rabensklippe, Burgberg

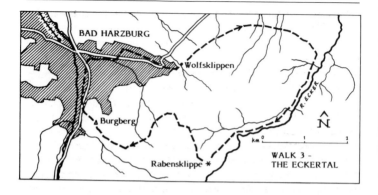

WALK 3 –
THE ECKERTAL

Route description: From the Ilsenburger road 200m past the Berufs Schule, just before the steep hairpin bend, take the lane Ilsenburger Stieg on the right, marked with a blue spot (50D) which climbs steeply past the last houses and out into the forest, past the Wolfsklippen (Wolf crags) bearing left and eventually contouring round the hillside for about 4km, with fine views from the edge of the Harz mountains northwards across the Harz foreland, before descending, above Stapelberg, into the Ecker valley.

This track through the valley alongside the little River Ecker (red triangle waymark 11G) follows what used to be the old Iron Curtain. You pass a paper and cardboard mill, as the valley curves westwards.

At a junction, take the higher path to the right, 20B which zigzags its way above the Hausmannsklippe; keep ahead with the waymarks to the Rabensklippe (Raven's crag) with its inn.

From here take the track heading due north 20F waymarked with a blue triangle which follows the ridge to another crossroads; left here along 20E marked with a blue bar on white. Follow this as it heads westwards past the Kreuz des Deutschen Ostens - a memorial to the fallen of East Germany - a fine viewpoint over Bad Harzburg. The track follows the ridge round and down into the little Stübchental. Follow the signs (blue spot) via Antonius Platz to the Große Burgberg (482m) with its ruined castle, fine views, refreshments and cable car should you decide to save the strain of a steep descent into Bad Harzburg.

Otherwise go via the Kleiner Burgberg ahead which also has a ruined fort before descending steeply into Krodotal with the centre of Bad Harzburg ahead.

Points of interest:

Bad Harzburg: One of the Harz's most famous resorts, Bad Harzburg recently had the centenary of its incorporation, but the town itself is generally believed to be considerably older. Its brine and mineral springs and good climate and its attractive situation on the northern slopes of the Harz mountains helped to make its reputation as an elegant resort where Russian archdukes, the King of Siam and even Otto von Bismarck were once among its regular visitors. It is still one of the four most important spa resorts in the Harz with an elegant shopping street, casino, coffee houses, and a splendid choice of hotels. There is also a music festival and horse racing week. A cable car to the summit of the Burgberg and a choice of walks make this an excellent centre for the northern Harz.

*   *   *

WALK 4: RAMMELSBERG AND THE SCHALKE 26/10/10
Goslar to Hahnenklee

This walk gives an opportunity to visit the remarkable Rammelsberg Mine Museum, followed by typical Harz landscape of forest tracks, long views and a series of lakes leading into Goslar's twin resort of Hahnenklee.

Distance:	16km (10 miles)
Time:	5 hours plus time to visit the mines.
Public transport:	Train to Goslar. Bus 2434 from Hahnenklee (or Auerhahn Inn) back to Goslar.
Parking:	Goslar
Map:	Naturpark Harz 1:50,000
Refreshment facilities:	Rammelsberg (Maltmeisterturm), Auerhahn Inn, Hahnenklee.

Route description: From Goslar Station walk through the magnificent town centre to the Marktplatz, heading south-westwards along

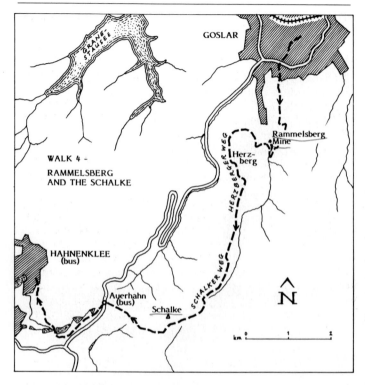

Bergstraße to where it meets the ring road, Clausthaler Straße, crossing into Rammelsberger Straße, almost opposite.

On the left-hand side is an advertisement pillar; to the side of this steps lead up into a narrow alleyway. Take this alleyway, past allotment gardens. This joins a narrow lane leading southwards past the youth hostel. Follow this tarmac road (green spot waymark - 23G) as it climbs uphill then hairpins round steeply into beech woods; an unmarked woodland path cuts off the bend. This leads up to the Maltmeisterturm, a magnificent viewpoint, now converted to a small restaurant.

Just past the Maltmeisterturm, a narrow path bears off to the right and descends past old workings down to the thousand year-old Rammelsberg Mine Museum; the entrance to the Museum (open daily) is along the lane to the right.

The route continues back along the lane from the Museum going steeply uphill, soon passing the dam and small lake which provided water to power the mines - now a swimming and boating lake and lido.

A track leads around the far side of the lake; keep right along the woodland and lakeside path, continuing through the woods with fine views of the mine buildings terraced up the hillside. Where the path ends at a forest track, turn left and follow the track uphill. Keep straight ahead steadily climbing up the Herzberg, ignoring junctions until the track joins a broader path waymarked with a red triangle, the Herzberger Way, 1F.

Walking is easy now through mainly coniferous forests around the Herzberg hill. The route gradually makes its way through a saddle of the hills, the valley Wintertal appearing on the right beyond the Kellerköpfe. Keep with the red triangle route now known as the Schalkerweg as it climbs the ridge. At the junction turn right to the summit of the Schalke where as well as military installations, a relic of the Cold War, you'll find a viewing tower with steps to allow you to enjoy panoramic views of the surrounding hills. Turn right along the track which is also the access road to the military installation, following it downhill to the main road from Clausthal-Zellerfeld where there is a large car park and a popular walker's inn, the Auerhahn - or Capercaille - as well as a bus back to Goslar.

Cross the road and continue along a track waymarked with a red spot 1D which follows a headland above a series of small Teichs or ponds, developed to provide water power for the mines, down into the somewhat extended village and resort of Hahnenklee. Buses back to Goslar go from outside the post office.

Points of interest:

Goslar: see Walk 5

The Rammelsberg Mine: According to legend, the rich Rammelsberg mine near Goslar was discovered in the tenth century, when the horse of a local knight called Ramm unearthed nuggets of silver on the hillside as it scratched restlessly at the ground with its hooves.

The knight reported the find to the Emperor who rewarded him greatly and named the Rammelsberg after him.

The Rammelsberg mine contains many early examples of mining technology such as medieval spoil tips, extensive levels or tunnels with tramways for the conveyance of ore, water wheels and power conveyance systems, as well as the remarkable Feuergezäher Vault clad in slate with slightly rounded Gothic arches, and the delightful Maltmeister tower. This tower used to house a large bell which tolled the start and ending of the mine's work shifts in the sixteenth century. This is now in the Goslar Museum. Finally closed in 1988, the Rammelsberg Mine is now a major regional mining museum.

Hahnenklee: Set amid rolling hills and attractive woodlands, Hahnenklee's wooden church in Norwegian style is a key feature with the warm tones of its wooden interior and beautifully carved pulpit making a very resonant atmosphere. Hahnenklee is now part of the Goslar district and is a spa and winter sports resort, Hahnenklee-Bochwiese. There is a cable car to the summit of the nearby Bocksberg. The Harzklub have a small museum in the former Town Hall.

✳   ✳   ✳

WALK 5: AROUND THE GRANESTAUSEE
Goslar circular

A combination of easy lakeside and forest rambling around the Grane reservoir, one of the largest of several reservoirs in the Harz Nature Park

Distance:	18km (12 miles)
Time:	5½ hours
Public transport:	Train to Goslar; the walk can be shortened by about 4km by linking to Wolfshagen (bus to Goslar).
Parking:	Goslar
Map:	Naturpark Harz 1:50,000, or Goslar Wanderkarte 1:30,000
Refreshment facilities:	Goslar

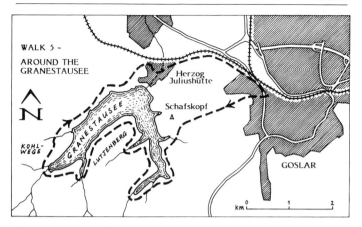

WALK 5 –
AROUND THE
GRANESTAUSEE

∧
N

KOHL-
WEGE

GRANESTAUSEE

Herzog
Juliushütte

Schafskopf
△

LUTJENBERG

GOSLAR

km 0   1   2

Route description: From Goslar Station Square turn right along the main road B82 beyond the Square north-westwards towards Langelsheim. About 200m beyond the railway bridge take the road left, again going under a railway bridge along a road signed am Nordberg and past a car park to where a forest track bears off to the right. Take the path which leads left off this along a grassy forest clearing, heading up along the ridge past waterworks buildings. Keep straight ahead over the brow of the ridge of the Nordberg. At a junction go right, but almost immediately left along a path over the summit of the ridge, the Schafskopf, before following it around to the left and curving into the little Lüdeckental and to a junction of tracks. Turn sharp right here along a path marked with a green triangle which leads down to and along the bank of the southern arm of the Granestausee reservoir.

Green triangle waymarks (2Q) now take you along quiet tracks or reservoir lanes around the shores of the reservoir. Keep right at the junction with Schüßeltal, following the southern tip of the reservoir over the Granebach stream that gives the lake its name, before heading north on the Rundweg across a series of headlands and bays, including a little dam over the Schwarzbach. There's a particularly fine view from the Lutjenberg, before the track heads south-westwards, this time crossing the Wienbach, and then past a shelter and over the Varleybach along an asphalted track heading north-eastwards, climbing above the lake.

Route 2J, joining from the left, leads from Wolfhagen, about 3km to the west; otherwise it continues past another fine viewpoint before joining a section of the Harz-Netherlands long distance path (1H white St Andrews cross on white ground) as it approaches Goslar.

At this point the track leads over the dam at the north-eastern corner of the reservoir before turning north-east towards the railway line from Goslar. Turn right at the railway line to follow the railway around the edge of the Hüttenwald into Goslar.

Points of interest:

Goslar: One of the most elegantly beautiful towns of the Harz, Goslar has a long and rich history. It was the seat of the German Holy Roman Emperors who reigned from the Kaiserpfalz built by Henry III in the eleventh century (restored in the nineteenth). Silver from the nearby Rammelsberg (Walk 4) enabled Henry to mint his own coins and enabled Goslar to become a great trading centre and one of the founders of the Hanseatic League, and a stronghold of medieval Christianity, culture and learning.

Of the ancient cathedral, only the Dom Vorhalle dating from 1150 remains and the Kaiserstuhl which was used by Kaiser Wilhelm I in 1871 to open the first Reichstag in Berlin when Germany was united.

Goslar's medieval core boasts about a thousand half timbered houses beautifully restored where necessary and many fine churches, once as many as forty-seven, but still twenty-three, among them the Markt Kirche with its Romanesque glass and two handsome towers. The Town Hall in the market square has a spectacular Huldigungssaal, originally the council chamber, where its painted walls and ceilings form a fitting backcloth to such treasures as the thirteenth-century jewelled Book of the Gospels and the Bergkanne, a superb example of Goslar silversmith's work.

The market place has a chiming clock with mechanical figures of medieval and modern miners who parade each hour whilst the central fountain in the square contains a gilded imperial eagle, the town's symbol. Among splendid carvings to be enjoyed on buildings are the Dukatenmannchen on the Kaiser Worth (originally belonging to a wealthy guild and dating from 1494) who produces golden coins in a somewhat unorthodox fashion and the much loved Butterhanne, a charming if uninhibited milkmaid to be seen on the Haus zum Brusttuch.

Granestausee: This reservoir which contains 45 million cubic metres of water is the second largest reservoir in the western Harz. It provides drinking water for several important towns and cities in Niedersachsen such as Hildesheim, Salzgitter, Wolfsburg and Braunschweig. With its setting in the forested hills, the lake creates fine effects of light and reflection from many vantage points on this circular walk.

✳   ✳   ✳

WALK 6: THE ODERTEICH
Torfhaus to St Andreasberg

A walk through forest and by reservoir to explore the central Oberharz Nature Reserve, with some spectacular scenery, rich in geological and wildlife interest.

Distance:	12km (8 miles)
Time:	4 hours
Public transport:	Bus 2422 from Bad Harzburg or Braunlage to Torfhaus (connections from Goslar); return on 2432 from St Andreasberg to Goslar; bus 65 from Andreasberg to Braunlage
Parking:	Goslar or Braunlage then as above
Map:	Naturpark Harz 1:50,000
Refreshment facilities:	Torfhaus, Oderteich, Renberger Grabenhaus, St Andreasberg

Route description: From Torfhaus main car park, head southwards along the main road to Braunlage for about 300m to where path 12C the Märchenweg or Fairy Tale way heads south-westwards, waymarked with a green triangle. As the track contours the hillside

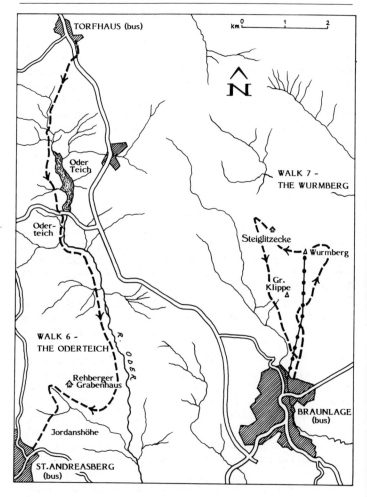

above a shallow stream, the path (still green triangle) heads down the hillside into the headwaters of the Oderteich, joining another route, at a picnic place; keep right at the head of the reservoir. Now follow the path, yellow spot waymark (18E), around the western bank of the reservoir, eventually reaching the head of the dam at the Clausthal Road B242 where there's a car park and inn.

From here take the track 15D (blue triangle waymark), signed to St Andreasberg. This follows the western rim of the narrow Oder valley, keeping right at a junction of tracks, and climbing steeply above the valley to follow it as it heads southwards. Part of it is a Geological Trail. This goes by a series of crags around the edge of the Rehberg, from where the route curves westwards to the Rehberger Grabenhaus inn and car park. Follow the road down the hillside in the same direction, keeping with the blue triangle 15D as the track contours above the steep valley turning southwards and heading into the open, mining landscape of St Andreasberg directly ahead.

Points of interest:

Torfhaus: As its name implies Torfhaus was where turf or peat was cut to provide fuel for the mining industry. It has for many years become a starting point for the most popular route up the Brocken, acquiring a large car park for the thousands of coaches and cars that come here. Before the Iron Curtain came down, there was a small Border Museum.

St Andreasberg: With its steep, narrow streets St Andreasberg, one of the Harz's seven mining towns which grouped themselves together for mutual support, is the highest town in the Harz. It contains the steepest main street of any town in Germany. It was founded by miners from Mansfeld at the end of the fifteenth century, silver and iron mining being its living for some centuries, and has typical clapboard houses, but is now a popular tourist centre; its elevated site and open views making it an ideal starting point for some outstanding walks. The former Samson Silver Mine, visited by Goethe in 1777, is now a major tourist attraction. There is also an extremely popular 500m "Superrutschbahn" or slide, and a chairlift to the summit of the Matthias Schmidt Berg. A long established Winterfest is held annually in St Andreasberg.

The Oderteich, passed on this walk, is Germany's oldest reservoir.

✳   ✳   ✳

WALK 7: THE WURMBERG
Braunlage circular

Though the Wurmberg isn't as high or as famous as The Brocken, it remains a popular summit and is easily enjoyed on this circular walk from the resort of Braunlage

Distance:	10km (6 miles)
Time:	4 hours
Public transport:	Braunlage is served by buses from Bad Harzburg (2422) - connections from Goslar - and Schierke and Elend Stations (84) and also from Bad Sachsa (2423).
Parking:	Braunlage; there is car park close to the cable car terminus to the summit.
Map:	Naturpark Harz 1:50,000. Route Map p62
Refreshment facilities:	Braunlage, Rodelhaus, Wurmberg summit

Route description: From the Braunlage bus terminus, head to the cable car terminal buildings to the right of which a waymarked path, red dot 35K, climbs up the hillside, going parallel to the cables, crossing underneath them and past the Kleine Klippe and up to the Rodel Wirtshaus inn.

The 35K now veers steeply to the north-east shoulder of the mountain, climbing sharply up to the serpentine way which ascends to the summit via the prehistoric Hexentreppe - Witches' Steps - to enjoy its magnificent views of the The Brocken and surrounding peaks and across into the former East Germany over the still physically visible Iron Curtain.

Leave the summit along the tarmac track heading north-westwards from the military buildings (35H, 35J), still with the red dot waymark to the Stieglizecke with its shelter and granite boulders.

After another 250m you reach a sharp corner; turn left along a pleasanter, greener way known as the Sackweg. This track contours

Oberharz: Goslar

Oberharz: Walking in the Okertal
Walkers on the Mausefalle above Okertal

around the slopes of the mountainside, descending to the Große Wurmberg Klippe, another fine example of a typical Harz granite "woolsack" tor.

Directly ahead is the Rodel Wirtshaus and the route 35K back to the centre of Braunlage.

Points of interest:

Braunlage: Already in 1227 there are records of iron mining and smelting in the area around Braunlage, and this industry continued throughout the centuries with silver, copper, cobalt and manganese in addition. Ample timber resources in the area meant that Braunlage was also able to supply timber and charcoal for mining and smelting. Just as the various ores were becoming depleted, mining became superseded by the tourist industry.

There is an excellent network of footpaths and it is also a good centre for winter sports. The first North German Ski Club was founded here.

The Wurmberg: The Wurmberg was in prehistoric times the site of an ancient Iron Age settlement, surviving features include the terraces on the eastern slopes and the Hexentreppe used on this walk.

Sadly, during the Cold War the Wurmberg became for the United States and NATO what the Brocken was for the Soviet Union and the Warsaw Pact - a major electronic information gathering point - and its tall radar tower, a notable landmark rivalled and challenged its near neighbour. Its tower takes the mountain's summit comfortably over the 1,000m mark. It is now a rambling and winter sports centre with restaurant and full facilities. Use of the cable car to avoid the steep climb will cut the distance of this walk approximately by half.

WALK 8: ST ANDREASBERG TO BAD LAUTERBERG OVER THE GROßER KNOLLEN

A classic forest ramble over ridge and through valley to link two popular West Harz resorts.

Distance:	17km (10½ miles)
Time:	5 hours
Public transport:	Bus 2432 from Goslar to St Andreasberg; 2433 from Bad Lauterberg to St Andreasberg; certain buses provide a through link to Goslar. Rail services from Bad Lauterberg to Herzberg, Nordheim.
Parking:	St Andreasberg
Map:	Naturpark Harz 1:50,000
Refreshment facilities:	St Andreasberg, Bad Lauterberg

Route description: From St Andreasberg bus station turn right to take the well marked path over the summit of the little Glockenberg, immediately to the south of the town, giving fine views of this former mining village and summer resort.

Descend to join the forest path, waymarked with a red spot (28B) as it drops into a steep gully; look for a narrow path near the bottom of the gorge which cuts off the corner, zigzagging down to the main road at Silberhütte.

Turn right up the road, but soon after it crosses the bridge look for a narrow path on the left, still 28B which climbs a steep gully at the side of Mühlenkopf. Follow it to the brow of the hill bearing right as it joins a forest track, but going left at the junction.

This track continues to climb, forking right at a junction with a red triangle waymark, and curving uphill for another 2km. At the next junction, take the red triangle waymarked path which follows a narrow and increasingly lovely forest path away from the track, following the ridge along the Aschenhalbe, the forest opening out to deciduous woods with small clearings with scattered shrubs and crags and fine open views.

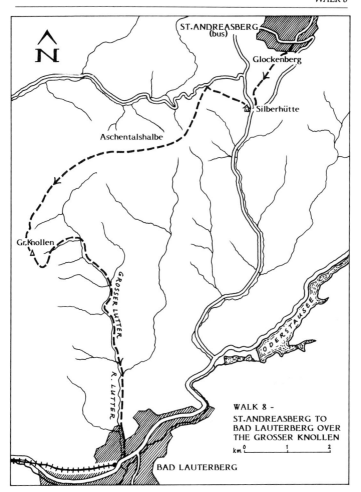

WALK 8 -
ST.ANDREASBERG TO
BAD LAUTERBERG OVER
THE GROSSER KNOLLEN

Continue over the summit, then descend sharply to join a track carrying European long distance route E8 which goes over a saddle before climbing steeply up to the summit of the Großer Knollen (687m) where there's a small viewing tower and inn offering welcome refreshment.

There is a choice of routes down to Bad Lauterberg or Scharzfeld from here, but a contrasting valley route leads to the left with the green spot waymark (13Q) which twists sharply round past old mine workings and back in the reverse direction along a lower track before a narrow track branches to the right down Knollental - signed Bad Lauterberg. Waymarking is not completely clear here and a little care is required.

Gradually the valley broadens out and becomes a wider forest track between tall walls of pine, with the track following the stream, the Grade Lutter. It is easy, fast walking now along the valley, meeting several side valleys to Kupferhütte where interpretive boards indicate the site of old copper workings and ponds. Straight ahead are the outskirts of Bad Lauterberg. Bus and railway stations are at the bottom of the town, though buses also leave the Postplatz in the town centre.

Points of interest:

St Andreasberg: see Walk 6

Bad Lauterberg: The name of this south Harz resort comes from a castle built by Count Sigibo from Schazfels on the Lutter or Lauter Berg, the site of the present renamed Haus Berg above the town. However it was copper mining which flourished between the fifteenth and the early nineteenth centuries that developed this town, as remains passed on this walk will testify. But in 1839 within a few years of the mines closing, the local doctor, Ernst Ritscher, founded the cold water baths, later Kneipp baths which established the town's reputation as a spa and inland resort. Water sports on the nearby Oder Reservoir add to walking and winter sports for the resort's continuing success.

✳   ✳   ✳

<h2 align="center">WALK 9: WEST HARZ MINING HERITAGE</h2>
Wildemann, Clausthal-Zellerfeld, Bad Grund

Lead, silver, copper and iron mining have left a profound impact on the Harz landscape and Harz towns, which despite decades of renaturing, still gives a distinctive character to many of the upland resorts.

Distance:	15km (9¹/₂ miles)
Time:	4¹/₂ hours
Public transport:	Bus 2408 from Goslar, Clausthal Zellerfeld and Altenau to Wildemann Mine Museum (Banhhof). Return on 2434 from Bad Grund via Clausthal-Zellerfeld to Goslar.
Parking:	Park in Goslar or Clausthal-Zellerfeld and catch the bus as above.
Map:	Naturpark Harz 1:50,000
Refreshment facilities:	Wildemann, Zellerfeld, Clausthal, Untere Innerste, Bad Grund

Route description: Take time to explore the small Mining Museum at Wildemann known as "19 Lachter Stollen".

The walk begins along a path which leaves from the main road close to the museum, 7C, waymarked with a green triangle and signed to Zellerfeld. This crosses the Innerste river and climbs a steep hill to the immediate east of the town, zigzagging up its summit and a shelter, known as the Schöne Aussicht - fine view. Path 7C then heads eastwards, descending the hill and climbing a ridge at the other side before joining a track which leads over yet another hillock directly into the edge of Zellerfeld, past a couple of

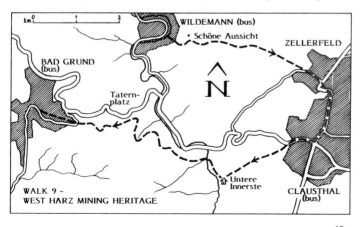

small ponds.

Keep in the same direction to the centre of Zellerfeld to the main road through the town, turning southwards down into the valley which separated the two hill towns, past the information centre in the old station and climbing uphill into Clausthal along the main street (B241) with its shops and cafes. Continue as far as Clausthal's remarkable wooden church before turning right at the busy crossroads and following the B242 towards Bad Grund, but after around 500m look for the path 2C (red triangle) signed for Bad Grund which branches off left soon ascending another small hill and viewpoint with a shelter, the Hüttenkopf.

Leave the hill in the same direction, curving southwards towards the little pond, the Kleine Clausthaler Teich, below to join a track from the pond leading to Untere Innerste where there's a car park and an inn. The route follows the little valley northwards before plunging on a path (2B - red triangle) which heads westwards, but keeps its height above the valley, following a ridge round and contouring above another little valley before bearing northwards again and around yet another steep hillside to a car park on the road to Bad Grund.

Keep on route 2B with the red triangle as it heads westwards, past old mine workings before joining other tracks which lead into the centre of Bad Grund. Buses back to Clausthal-Zellerfeld and Goslar leave from the little bus station (ZOB) in the town centre.

Points of interest:

Wildemann: This little former mining town, and one of the seven Harz mining towns forming an industrial entity, is set deep in the Innerste and Grumbach valleys, earing the nickname "little Tyrol" in the past because of its distinctive topography. It's now a thriving spa and winter sports centre, but the Mine Museum keeps a link with the town's industrial past.

Clausthal-Zellerfeld: Clausthal and Zellerfeld, close neighbours on nearby hilltops, were formally joined together in 1924, having for centuries been two of the seven original Harz mining towns which had grouped together to further their industrial and manufacturing interests. Zellerfeld was originally a twelfth-century Benedictine foundation and gained importance from about 1500 through its

Mine locomotive and waterwheel, Wildemann

mines. The town was rebuilt in the baroque style after a great fire, and one of its most striking buildings is the baroque Bergapotheke. There is also an interesting mining museum, Das Oberharzer Bergwerkmuseum, which is situated in the centre of Zellerfeld.

Clausthal has a very striking all wooden parish church built in 1642 and the largest of its kind in Germany with seats for 2,200 people. The mining offices are in baroque style partly in wood, partly in slate and there are two old mining cottages in the Zehntnerstraße.

Bad Grund: Originally the oldest of the seven Harz mining towns, it is also known as the town of the five valleys. Of the seventeen original mines only one (in 1993) is still working. The Mining Museum "Rohstoffqueller Harz" is operated in partnership with this mine in Bad Grund.

Surrounded by dense deciduous and spruce forests, this town, which became a Bad or spa in the nineteenth century, is particularly attractive, with its half-timbered houses and red tiled roofs. The Johannisfest (24th June) and the Walpurgisfest (30th April) are celebrated annually. Close to the town (and linked by waymarked paths) are the Iberger Caves and the Iberger Albrecht Turm.

✳   ✳   ✳

WALK 10: SOUTH-WEST HARZ
Herzberg to Osterode

A walk linking two attractive towns in the south-west corner of the Oberharz Nature Park.

Distance:	16km (10 miles)
Time:	5 hours
Public transport:	Train from Northeim and Nordhausen, and from Seesen via Osterode (rail connections from Bad Harzburg and Goslar), and Bad Lauterberg; bus 2458 also links Seesen Station, Osterode and Herzberg and operates as a rail replacement service at off peak times - weekdays and evenings.

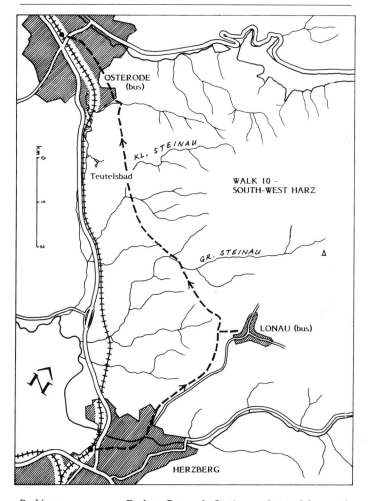

Parking:	Park at Osterode Station and travel forward to Herzberg by train or bus.
Map:	Naturpark Harz 1:50,000
Refreshment facilities:	Herzberg, Lonau, Osterode

Route description: From Herzberg Station, walk towards the town centre, taking the first road left past the information office, turning left with the blue triangle waymarked route signed for Lonau. This crosses the Sieber river and heads northwards along a track into the Lonau Valley. Soon past a picnic and barbecue area, the blue triangle route 14A ascends to the edge of the forest below the Amtmannsberg up the Lonau Valley. Keep ahead with yellow and blue triangles; at a crossroads and shelter, turn right into the little forest resort of Lonau. A bus returns from here to Herzberg, should you decide to cut the walk short for any reason.

Retrace your steps as far as this crossroads, this time keeping due west with path 14G and a red triangle, climbing steadily up the hillside and contouring around the ends of a series of ridges, still with the red triangle, heading due north-westwards.

You cross into the valley of the Großer Steinau, and then past the Kastanienplatz (square of chestnut trees), keeping height over crossing tracks before descending into the Kleiner Steinau valley. 14G threads its way over more crossing tracks climbing out of the Steinau valley over another thickly wooded ridge, gradually losing height into the main Sieber valley with the Teufelsbad - a marshland nature reserve - below the hillside on your immediate left.

As the path approaches the outskirts of Osterode, crossing the Arenke, 14G crosses either path leading into the town centre of Osterode, the higher route which joins European Path E6 being slightly less urban.

Points of interest:

Herzberg: Herzberg on the southern edge of the Harz is a busy market town and resort which is a useful starting point for excursions into the Harz. Its castle, founded by Barbarossa, was later acquired by Henry the Lion and the powerful Guelf family and it also was the original headquarters of the house of Hannover. This half-timbered building has a most strikingly beautiful clock tower.

Lonau: This little resort has grown up around a former iron mining settlement which was already well established in 1615; there is a choice of hotels and guest houses, inns and cafes, and it provides a useful starting point for a series of good well waymarked walks.

Osterode: Although already a mining centre by the mid-fifteenth century, Osterode was actually established in medieval times and has some fine old buildings, narrow streets, half-timbered houses and a Renaissance town hall to bear witness to its origin. It is one of the largest of the Harz towns with ample accommodation and is a useful access point into the eastern side of the region.

THE MITTLEHARZ (Middle Harz)
Walks 11-20

The glory of the central Harz is undoubtedly the Brocken itself and the Hochharz National Park, not perhaps the still-ravaged Brocken summit but the great, brooding peak as a whole with its magnificent open areas of woodland and high moorland with those distinctive gnarled tree stumps, granite "woolsack" Klippen and the cotton grass with its contrasting white plumes.

Best centres to explore this lovely region are almost anywhere on the Harzquerbahn, but points such as Drei Annen Hohne (on the National Park boundary), Schierke, Elend, Sorge or Benneckenstein are all ideal, as is Wernigerode itself with all its facilities and architectural splendours.

Former watch tower, Brocken summit

WALK 11: THE BROCKEN
Schierke to Brocken Summit

The classic route from Schierke to the summit of the Harz's most celebrated mountain. For a longer walk this can usefully be combined with Walk 12 back to Drei Annen Hohne or back to Schierke.

Distance:	8km (5 miles), plus 2km panorama walk around the summit.
Time:	2^1/$_2$ hours plus time to explore the summit
Public transport:	Train (Brockenbahn) to Schierke; return from Brocken summit. Also direct bus service to Schierke from Wernigerode (H.257) and Braunlage (84).
Parking:	Schierke Railway Station (1.5km east of town), returning by train.
Map:	Wandern im Mittleren Harz
Refreshment facilities:	Schierke Station, Brocken Summit. Cafes, outdoor kiosks (including the famous Brocken "Goulasch cannons" serving hot pea soup).

Route description: From Schierke Station cross the railway track and turn left along the "Bahn Parallelweg" (green triangle). Keep ahead on a long, straight steadily ascending track through forest alongside the railway, with views of the Wurmberg through the trees, past a crossing of paths at Schlungsklippe (3km); continue with the railway parallel track to Eckerloch - a narrow gully and steep mountainside, from where the railway curves to the left around the shoulder of the mountain ridge. The footpath, however, turns sharply to the right alongside a stream, narrowing and climbing steeply uphill, with sections over wooden duckboards along the way to reduce erosion. It ascends through more open woodland to join a broad tarmac lane, the Brockenstraße.

Turn left here and cross the re-emerging railway line to join the Goetheweg (Walk 14) by the shelter huts and horsebus terminus from Schierke, a surviving portion of border fence - retained as a

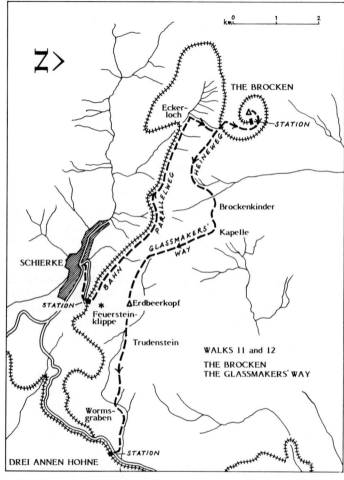

grim memorial. Follow this busy, broad track as it curves up to the Brocken Summit. A 2km walk around the former perimeter fence gives superb views in all directions, passing surviving watchtowers, the television masts and telecommunications centre, the existing Russian Army Base (due to close in 1995) and the crags known as the

Hexenaltar - The Witches Altar.

Return trains to Schierke and Drei Annen Hohne leave the Brocken Station; check departure times in advance; alternatively the first section of Walk 12 can be used as far as Brockenbett to make an attractive circular walk back to Schierke (18km).

Points of interest:

Schierke: Situated in the Elendtal, the top end of the valley of the Kalte Bode, its name evolved from Schrikeren or Schiere meaning a bare oak tree, reflecting its origin in wood cutting and charcoal burning. In later years, its inhabitants worked in the smelting works or hired themselves out as Brocken guides when it became fashionable to climb the summit, the town soon establishing itself as a walking and winter sports centre. During the Cold War Schierke found itself within the restricted boundary area between the two Germanies and a special permit was needed to enter and leave the area, access being largely restricted to party trusties and the secret police.

The Brocken Summit: The National Park Information Centre in a converted radar station dome contains material both on the natural history and the recent grim story of the Iron Curtain and activities of the infamous Border Police. (A new Centre is about to be opened.) There are tours of the Brocken Garden (an alpine garden) at 11am each day with a commentary in German. For full information about the Brocken, see Part One.

WALK 12: THE GLASSMAKERS WAY
Brocken Summit to Drei Annen Hohne

One of the loveliest of walks through the Hochharz National Park, with some spectacular views of this Brocken summit.

Distance:	13km (8 miles)
Time:	4 hours
Public transport:	Brockenhbahn from Drei Annen Hohne or Wernigerode
Parking:	National Park Car Park at Drei Annen Hohne
Map:	Wandern im Mittleren Harz. Route Map p78
Refreshment facilities:	Brocken Summit, Drei Annen Hohne

Route description: From the Brocken summit (see Walk 11), follow the broad track, the main Goetheweg, due south, curving down the hillside past protected areas to the railway crossing. Keep ahead here along the main tarmac road, the Brockenstraße (waymarked with a green St Andrews cross), over the railway crossing and parallel to the hillside, the ancient woodlands and nature reserve below Heinrichshöhe for 3km to where the road curves left into a broad gully and natural saddle in the mountainside, Am Brocken Bett, at a crossing of tracks.

If you are returning to Schierke, turn right here descending the main track down the gully (green cross again) along the old Bobsled route leading directly into Schierke; turn left along the Bahnparallelweg (green triangle) if you are heading for Schierke Station.

For the main route to Drei Annen, continue along the road curving right, but look for a narrower track on the left signed with the green cross (an alternative loop), the Glasshüttenweg, literally the Glassworks Way, or more idiomatically perhaps the Glassmakers Way. Almost immediately by the rest hut on the left another waymarked, but much narrower path, signed Brockenkinder, leads past and around the outside of a cottage, still with the green cross waymark, into a lovely area of scattered rocks, bilberries and trees,

Brockenkinder

with superb views of the Brocken Summit - a lovely place to sit and picnic.

From here the path, still well waymarked, bears to the right and ascends through scrub wood and crags to the Brockenkinder - the Brocken children, a group of typical "woolsack" weather worn granite crags or tors.

Keep on the narrow waymarked (green triangle) path now heading eastwards through the woods and across a narrow dip to the Kapelle - Chapel - ahead, another even taller group of wind-carved crags. From here the path narrows and needs to be carefully followed, scrambling between and over boulders (look for waymarks) through the forest down to the gravel track below, the Glasshüttenweg once more.

Easy, level walking now through dense forest with the occasional clearing for about 2km to where, on the right, a narrow grassy path leads across to Ahrensklippe, a tall, granite crag with iron ladders up to its summit from where superb views across Schierke and the Elend Valley can be enjoyed.

Return along the path which forks right to rejoin the Glashüttenweg as it curves northwards. Now comes a slightly complex junction where you should follow the yellow cross waymarks to the Erdbeerkopf - Strawberry Top or Summit - along a narrow path through deep forest on the right, turning almost immediately left, at another junction, to head due east and ascending to the summit of a hillock whose wire ropeway and clearance gives fine views from a strategically placed bench.

The route continues directly ahead, descending steeply through deciduous woods, mainly beech, finally joining a track, the Glashüttenweg, coming in from the left. Follow the signs to Drei Annen Hohne, crossing the little River Wormke. Trudenstein, soon reached on the right, is another tall gritstone crag complete with staircase, again giving fine views, this time over a former explosives factory deep in the woods, and as far as Rübeland and its quarries to the east. Keep ahead to where the path joins a broader track (red dash waymark) and on to Drei Annen Hohne, a refreshment kiosk strategically positioned at the end of the path, the car park directly ahead, the station with its cafe and bar to the right.

Points of interest:

The Brocken: (see Walk 11 and Part One)

Brocken National Park: (see Part One)

The Glashüttenweg - Glassmakers Way. Glassmaking was an important industry in times past, using charcoal, quartz and sand. Tracks like this would have been used to transport raw materials or finished glassware.

Schierke: see Walk 11

Drei Annen Hohne: Drei Annen Hohne derives its name "drei Annen" - three Annas - from three ladies all called Anna and close relatives of a local aristocrat and landowner, while "Hohne" is another name for hill. Formerly an old mining area, with a standard gauge railway from Königshütte that served a low-level station whose refreshment room can still be seen, it is a useful starting point for a variety of walks, and the busy junction for Schierke and the Brockenbahn (excellent station refreshment room). Two fairly large hotels in the area provide a useful accommodation base on the edge of the National Park.

There is a National Park Information Centre in the main car park below the station.

✻　　✻　　✻

WALK 13: HEINRICH HEINE'S WAY
Brocken Summit to Ilsenburg

This walk replicates the journey made by poet Heinrich Heine in 1824 when he visited the Brocken and made his way through the beautiful Ilse Valley to Ilsenburg.

Distance:	17km (10$^1/_2$ miles)
Time:	5 hours
Public transport:	Brockenbahn to Brocken Summit, returning from Ilsenburg by train to Wernigerode
Parking:	Suggest Wernigerode (public car park near station), catching morning train to Brocken, and returning from Ilsenburg.

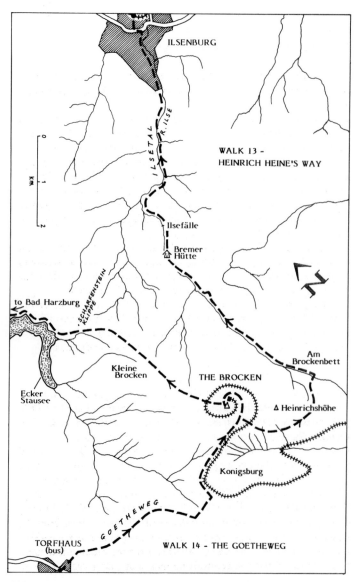

ILSENBURG

WALK 13 –
HEINRICH HEINE'S WAY

ILSETAL

R. ILSE

Ilsefälle

Bremer
Hütte

SCHARFENSTEIN
KLIPPE

to Bad Harzburg

Am
Brockenbett

Kleine
Brocken

THE BROCKEN

Δ Heinrichshöhe

Ecker
Stausee

Konigsburg

GOETHEWEG

TORFHAUS
(bus)

WALK 14 – THE GOETHEWEG

Map:	Wandern im Mittleren Harz
Refreshment facilities:	Brocken Summit, Ilsenburg

Route description: Leave the Brocken Summit along the Goetheweg, continuing along the Brockenstraße as far as Brockenbett (see Walk 12).

From here take the track on the left through the forest signed 55D Heineweg to Ilsenburg. This ascends the top of the Elend Valley and across the watershed, picking up the top end of the Ilse Valley.

Keep ahead at the crossroads with the Ilsenburg signs and green bar waymark, the track serpentining past the Kellbeck and other small streams through the forest. Continue past Oberer Meineckenburg along the section of path known as the Bremer Weg, before joining the track 9E (red triangle and red bar) past the Heine Memorial.

Turn right at the junction into the main Ilse valley, but almost immediately take the footbridge across the river to a narrower riverside path (blue and red bar waymarks) along the far side of the river. This is a particularly beautiful section of the Ilsetal.

The path continues below the famous Ilsenstein crag before eventually joining a broader track and tarmac lane into the outskirts of Ilsenburg and into the town centre. The railway station is about 1km to the north-east of the town on the Veckenstedt road.

Points of interest:

Heinrich Heine Way: One of Germany's greatest poets, Heinrich Heine (1797-1856), left a record of his journey in his *Harz Reise* published in 1826. This route from the summit of the Brocken through the Ilse valley is the route described by Heine.

Ilsenburg: The name Ilsenburg derives from the old German word for alder tree. The town owes its origin to what originally was a Benedictine foundation belonging to the Bishops of Halberstadt which eventually came to be owned by the counts of Stolberg-Wernigerode. The town at the point where the beautiful Ilse valley emerges from the Harz mountains, became well known from the sixteenth century onwards for its smelting and metal working industries and was visited by Peter the Great of Russia on account of its manufacturing interests. It remains a largely industrial town though a good point from which to explore the northern Harz.

The great German Romantic painter David Caspar Friedrich painted a celebrated view of the Ilsenstein passed on this walk.

✳   ✳   ✳

WALK 14: THE GOETHEWEG
Torfhaus to Bad Harzburg

In the footsteps of another famous German writer, Wolfgang von Goethe, tracing his famous ascent of the summit; a fine route off the summit is used to make a return to Bad Harzburg, a satisfying if strenuous day's walk.

Distance:	22km (14 miles)
Time:	7 hours
Public transport:	Bus 2422 (KVG) operates frequently between Bad Harzburg, Torfhaus and Braunlage, and route 84 links Schierke and Elend with Braunlage. Bus 86 links Bad Harzburg with Wernigerode.
Parking:	In Bad Harzburg, returning to Torfhaus on bus 2422; services continue until mid evening.
Map:	Wandern im Mittleren Harz. Route Map p84
Refreshment facilities:	Torfhaus, Brocken summit, Molkenhaus; Bad Harzburg

Route description: From the main car park and bus stop at Torfhaus from where you'll get a good view of the Brocken summit, follow the path at the side of the main Braunlage road southwards for about 250m to where the Goetheweg marked for the Brocken 10F (red spot in white triangle) bears off left down the valley of the Abbeygraben.

This is a busy, well used path and waymarking is good, making pathfinding easy enough. After 2km, having crossed the little River Abbe, the way bears right joining another track, and soon forks left, a stone marking the name of the route Goetheweg. Keep with the red spot waymark. This follows the edge of the forest, crossing the broad clearing in the forest which marked the old hostile border between the two Germanies. Part of the fence still remains (1993). The path now climbs steeply to join and turn left along the line of the now re-opened railway.

Until recently this path followed the trackbed of the railway line itself. Since the line was re-opened in 1992, a new path has been constructed alongside. Follow it as it climbs steadily uphill, curving eastwards on a steady ascent towards the distant summit. You are likely to see a train passing, though in the peak season diesels rather than steam locomotives are used to haul the packed trains.

The path and railway meet the broad tarmac Brockenstraße, by shelters and the terminal point of the horse drawn carriages from Schierke. Turn left along a surviving portion of fence with its commemorative plaque, following the Brockenstraße up to the mountain summit, the summit station and radar masts soon coming into view. This section of track is usually extremely busy with hundreds of people making the pilgrimage to the summit itself.

Unless you plan to return to Schierke or Drei Annen (see Walk 12), your route off the summit is to the north via the Hirtensteig - the Shepherd's Ascent (11C waymarked with a green bar). This crosses open moorland and scrub, soon recrossing the railway as it corkscrews round the summit ridge, heading directly along the long mountain ridge over the Brockenmoor and the ridge end known as the Little Brocken before plunging back into forest and the main descent.

Keep the same direction down the hillside, past Hermans Klippe and Bismarksklippe before eventually reaching after a little more than 4km from the Brocken a crossing track. Turn left here, still following 11C and the green bar waymark, going left again at the next junction, then right still with 11C around the Eckerstau - the Ecker Valley Reservoir.

Keep left around the reservoir before crossing the old border again. Turn right at the next junction, now taking 11J with the blue St Andrews cross which leads along the Ecker valley before bearing left with the blue cross to the Molkenhaus where there's a popular walkers' inn and cafe.

There is a choice of routes to Bad Harzburg, but the recommended

Plaque of Goethe, Brocken Summit

one is the Kaiserweg, 19C and marked with a blue spot, which follows the contours around above the Kalte valley, before swinging north-westwards along forest tracks to emerge at Bad Harzburg's "local mountain" the Großer Burgberg, complete with cable car service to shorten the end of the walk. Alternatively there are a choice of ways, perhaps northwards via the Kleine Burgberg down into the centre of Bad Harzburg with all its many facilities. The railway station is at the northern end of town, but buses also stop in the town centre.

Points of interest:

Gotheweg: This is the route first used by Johann Wolfgang von Goethe in his famous ascent of the Brocken in 1777, (see Part One). It is now perhaps the most popular and heavily used of all mountain walks in Germany, especially in the holiday months.
Brocken Summit: see Walk 11
Bad Harzburg: see Walk 3

✳   ✳   ✳

WALK 15: HOHNE KLIPPEN AND STEINERNE RENNE
Drei Annen Hohne to Steinerne Renne Station

Distance:	12km (7 miles)
Time:	3¹/₂ hours
Public transport:	Harzquerbahn to Drei Annen Hohne and from Steinerne Renne
Parking:	Park either at Drei Annen Hohne by National Park Centre or in Wernigerode.
Map:	Wandern im Mittleren Harz
Refreshment facilities:	Drei Annen Hohne, Steinerne Renne

Route description: From Drei Annen Hohne station exit turn right to the crossroads, then left along the track past a refreshment kiosk and past the sign into the Hochharz National Park. Follow the track past cottages, keeping straight ahead along with the red bar waymarks towards Hohne Klippen. After crossing the Wormsgraben and stream, fork right, still with the red bar waymark, to a track which ascends the hillside, bearing left at the next fork to climb steeply up the ridge past the Bärenklippen (Bear crags) onto and along the summit ridge of this rocky, partly bare, partly forested ridge.

Continue to the summit, Grenzklippe, with its Rest Hut. The way down is the path on the right marked with a red spot (55E) to the Ottofels. Follow this steeply down through the forest, on a path known as Beerensteig. You eventually reach a broad crossing track. Turn left here, still with the red spot, but where you reach a crossroads, turn right, with the blue spot, marked Ottofels.

Continue for about 1km, past young forest and up a narrower track path on the right, close to a small youth field centre, is Ottofels, or Otto's Crag. A path behind the hostel twists up to this high crag, which can be climbed by a series of metal stairs and rails to its viewing platform.

Return the same way to the main path, turning right along the track with the red spot waymark which bears now north-westwards through forest. Keep ahead until the path drops into a rocky gorge

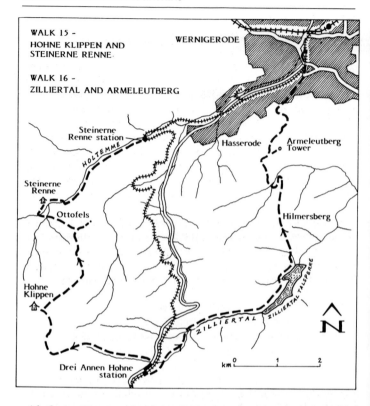

with the poetic name Steinerne Renne - perhaps best translated as stony gutter or stony runnel. There's a lovely period house above the gorge reached by footbridge across the gorge with an outdoor refreshment terrace above the waterfall and an indoor restaurant.

Path 11E continues down the southern side of the gorge, eventually joining the track in the forest by an old hydro-electric works. Ahead, and on your right at the far side of an astonishingly tight curve on the railway line, is the station. Should you wish to continue to the centre of Wernigerode through its twin village of Hasselrode, it's no more than about 5km - little more than an hour's level walk away.

Points of interest:

Drei Annen Hohne: see Walk 12

Ottofels is another of those remarkable wind carved gritstone crags which are such a feature of the Harz mountains. From here there are magnificent views across the rolling hilltops westwards back towards the Hohneklippen ridge with its great tree clearances, the Brocken beyond and down towards the thickly forested valley with Wernigerode to the north-east, its castle a prominent feature.

Steinerne Renne: At Steinerne Renne the fast flowing stream in this narrow ravine goes through beautiful woodland rich in wildlife. A small memorial to the victims of a slave labour factory which once existed by the riverside close to the station is a grim reminder of the atrocities which took place even in the Harz mountains during the Nazi era.

Steinerne Renne station is an excellent place from which to catch a train back to Drei Annen Hohne. Steam locomotives climbing this part of the route are working extremely hard and noisily to gain height before the long ascent to Drei Annen summit through Drangetal and its tunnel - the only one on the Harz network.

✳   ✳   ✳

WALK 16: ZILLIERTAL AND ARMELEUTBERG
Drei Annen Hohne to Wernigerode

Easy walk along the Zilliertal is a prelude to a short ascent and some magnificent views into the Harz foreland before a delightful ramble through oakwoods into one of the Harz's most famous and beautiful historic towns.

Distance:	14km (9 miles)
Time:	4 hours
Public transport:	Harzquerbahn to Drei Annen Hohne and from Wernigerode
Parking:	Wernigerode and catch the morning train to Drei Annen Hohne
Map:	Wandern im Mittleren Harz. Route Map p90

Refreshment facilities: Drei Annen Hohne, Armeleutberg
(Monday, Tuesday closed), Wernigerode

Route description: From Drei Annen Station exit through the tunnel at the end of the stationside platform to the main car park and National Park Centre. Turn right for a short distance at the end of the car park on the Elbingerode road, but look for the track on the left signed Wernigerode and via Zilliertal and waymarked with a red triangle.

Take this route as it follows the little Zillier stream, which soon joins a broader track, bearing right along the shallow valley: easy walking for nearly 3km before the track reaches and follows the edge of the Zillier reservoir, with a fine viewpoint where the track turns sharply round.

Soon the path descends past a reservoir works and a small car park and shelter. Keep ahead beyond this but as the track slopes even more sharply down, just to the right of a small reservoir building on the left, a track now slopes steeply uphill, with a half concealed red triangle waymark on the tree above. This is your route, climbing steeply out of the reservoir valley through older established and later newer forest, up to the summit of the Hilmersberg with a small shelter and picnic area on the summit ridge, a fine viewpoint, the Kaiserturm a landmark on the Armeleutberg on the ridge ahead.

Keep the same direction, with the red triangle ahead, the path curving round the northern edge of the Hilmersberg and joining a tarmac lane running through another hairpin around a narrow valley below. Keep ahead around the bend before forking left along a track uphill with the signs to Armeleutberg ahead. The track climbs a wooded slope past the Forestry Station to a junction and forest footpath noticeboard, with an impressive view across to the Brocken on the left.

Turn right following the track up to the Armeleutberg inn, continuing uphill for another 300 metres to the Kaiserturm, on the hill summit.

Return to the inn, immediately beyond which a narrow path, signed to Wernigerode, leads through the woods. This becomes a very beautiful path. Keep the same direction, following signs to the

Walkers near rest shelter, Hilmersberg

Organistenkopf (Organists's Head) and Stadt (city centre) with the green waymark, the path now contouring round through the most superb oakwoods, and with open views.

You emerge by some handsome suburban houses and gardens in the outskirts of Wernigerode. Turn left past gardens, then right downhill, and right again at the first junction into the town centre.

Points of interest:

Drei Annen Hohne: see Walk 12.

Kaiserturm: The Kaiserturm or Emperor's Tower, on the Armeleutberg, is a tall stone viewing tower, with a spiral staircase built to commemorate the Kaiser's Jubilee, and newly restored. From the summit there are magnificent, panoramic viewpoints across Wernigerode with its romantic hillside castle and into the fertile plains beyond.

Wernigerode: Records of the old walled town of Wernigerode, lying at the confluence of two Harz rivers, the Holtemme and the Zillierbach, date back to 961. Its strategic position along key trade routes across the northern Harz and Harz foreland aided its development and in 1291 it was granted the full status of a town. When the Counts of Wernigerode, its overlords, died without issue in 1429, the town and its environs passed into the hands of the Counts of Stolberg.

In later medieval times the town's prosperity increased with the rise of such industries as clothmaking, leather tanning, iron mining, papermaking and dyeing. By 1528 the old and expanding new towns had joined together, but the town had the usual share of plagues and large fires. Later industries were tile making, pottery, brewing as well as the timber and metal industries, while prior to World War II a large light engineering plant developed there. The modern industrial part of the town to the east with its tall tower blocks makes a dramatic contrast to the old town centre, luckily not destroying or even impinging on the historic core.

Wernigerode's medieval castle, rebuilt in the nineteenth century, overlooks the town from a rocky ridge. It is now a museum, the Feudalmuseum. The fourteenth-century Town Hall in the main square with its rich carving, coloured and gilded gables and pinnacled turrets is one of the finest in all Germany, looking for all the world like something out of a fairy tale. Originally the town hall was first mentioned as a Spelhus and was used both as courthouse and as a place where medieval entertainments took place.

The writer Herbert Löns christened Wernigerode "die bunte Stadt am Harz" - the colourful town in the Harz, and you can see why as you roam through its numerous streets with their rows of fine half timbered houses and shops, and richly carved public buildings. The Krummelaches Haus with its richly carved exterior dating from 1674 is typical of many architectural treasures. The fifteenth-century Gadenstadt house has some splendid detail while the Cafe Wien in Breite Straße has been a cake shop and cafe since the turn of the century. There is a small Harz museum in the Library just behind the town hall.

Though now an extremely busy and popular tourist centre, Wernigerode keeps its essential character. Situated as it is on the northern terminus of the Harzquerbahn and also on the main railway line to Magdeburg and Halberstadt, with bus links to Bad Harzburg, it is an excellent centre to explore much of both the Mittelharz and Unterharz.

✳   ✳   ✳

WALK 17: THREE VALLEYS
Drei Annen Hohne to Benneckenstein

A walk into a quieter part of the Harz Mountains, dominated by the central Harz forests, crossing over three steep river valleys down to the Warme Bode, with some fine views and excellent opportunities to enjoy wildlife and natural history.

Distance:	16km (10 miles)
Time:	5 hours
Public transport:	Harzquerbahn to Drei Annen Hohne, return from Benneckenstein (or Sorge).
Parking:	Hochharz National Park Car Park at Drei Annen Hohne and return by train.
Map:	Wandern im Mittleren Harz
Refreshment facilities:	Drei Annen, Mandelholz, Tanne (limited), Sorge, Benneckenstein

Route description: From Drei Annen Hohne National Park Centre, take the track which leaves the south-eastern corner of the car park (red spot and yellow bar waymark) and goes due east through forest before, after 1km, joining a broader track which curves south along the little valley of the Hirchenbach, eventually reaching a lavishly signed crossroads by a shelter, with a footbridge across the stream.

Follow the track marked by the yellow square waymark south-westwards, signed Mandelholz which curves around a low wooded hillock known as the Bastkopf. Keep ahead at the crossroads ignoring the Mandelholz signs, keeping with the yellow squares as the track descends westwards by dense forest plantations across Apelnhäu for another kilometre until you reach a broader track. Go left here but after around 80m, turn left again along a narrower track down the somewhat atmospheric ravine of Dammgrab, past the remains of a dam. Look for a footbridge on the right where a narrow path crosses the beck and passes old mine workings to emerge at the welcoming Mandelholz Inn (refreshments).

Opposite the inn is a large car park. A narrow path leaves its western end, at first parallel to the road and broadening, but after about 400m it bears left down, into and across the open valley below, to wind through the scrubland that forms the western tip of the Mandelholz reservoir. Keep ahead across a precarious little swing bridge over the Kalte Bode River, before ascending to a track below the forest. Turn left here following the green spot waymark and signs to Tanne.

After about 500m, this path turns sharp right, still marked for Tanne, into the forest, and now begins a long ascent through dense forest. Follow it uphill past a tall wooden shooting stand to a crossing track. Turn left, still with the Tanne signs, for about 100m, to another junction where a path, now fairly level, goes through dense woods, though with occasional enclosures, before the track descends into another valley, this time traversed by a stone track and the Spielbach stream.

Turn right for about 50m to a junction where the green spot waymarks directs you left, steeply uphill by the edge of the forest over the Ramsenhöhe, a hillock of scattered, open woodland and grass with magnificent views of the distant Brocken - an ideal picnic area on a fine day. Keep in the same direction, soon descending yet another valley with a stony track; cross it and go over a little footbridge ahead, to turn right along a parallel track in the woods for about 250m to a junction, turning right uphill to a broad, crossing track on the brow of the hill. Turn left, now gently descending by woods, soon passing open pasture (a wild game feeding area) and a small pond on the left; just before a crossroads take the path to the right signed to Tanne. This climbs through tall woods. Keep straight ahead at a junction eventually reaching open fields with impressive views across to wooded hills that flank the Warme Bode Valley; at a crossroads with an evocative memorial erected by local people to "our working forefathers and mothers" fork right, between meadows crossing a shallow valley to the village and small health resort of Tanne.

The path enters the top of the village; take the first lane, Linden Straße on the right past a small garden and memorial, keeping ahead at the next junction to where, past a large hostel, the lane peters out and becomes a lovely field track across the meadows. At

Unterharz: Quedlinburg Town Hall
Armeleuteberg - a view across the Weringerode

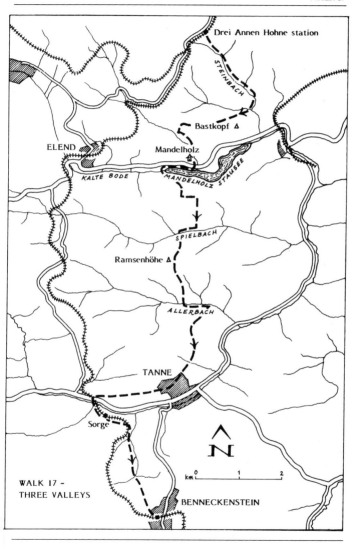

Drei Annen Hohne station

STEINBACH

Bastkopf ▲

ELEND

Mandelholz

KALTE BODE

MANDELHOLZ STAUSEE

SPIELBACH

Ramsenhöhe ▲

ALLERBACH

TANNE

Sorge

N

km 0   1   2

WALK 17 –
THREE VALLEYS

BENNECKENSTEIN

Unterharz: The Kaiserturm at Armeleuteberg

a junction, a narrow path signed to Sorge leads downhill to join the main road and across the Warme Bode River into the village of Sorge.

Walk through the village towards the station; an excellent cafe about 100m to the right of the station offers beautifully kept local Bockbeer, and you might wish to finish the walk here. Otherwise, it's about 3km to Benneckenstein, following the track (green square waymarks) beyond the station and parallel to the railway. This crosses the line and bears right with the railway, before leaving it to climb through the woods, a gentle ascent which passes a reed fringed pond close to the summit before emerging at Benneckenstein station (refreshments at the station cafe). The main part of the town, part tourist part industrial, lies 200m further on.

Points of interest:

Wildlife: This walk follows well waymarked tracks and paths deep into typical Central Harz Forest, and offers splendid opportunities to enjoy the area's wildlife at its best; whilst surveying it we encountered deer, a herd of moufflon, a wild boar and a wildcat seen from the return train, as well as ubiquitous buzzards over head and especially rich wildflowers in the open meadows.

Bergdamm: The former dam in the woods near Mandelholz provided waterpower for local lead and silver mines. Its sudden collapse more than a century ago caused devastating damage. The present Mandelholz reservoir forms part of a complex of reservoirs on the twin Bode and other rivers, serving the needs of a number of cities in Sachsen-Anhalt.

Tanne and Sorge: Tanne and Sorge are typical small Mittelharz resorts in the Warme Bode valley; Tanne clinging to the valley side has typical clapboard architecture and a small Kurpark and alpine garden, but Sorge closer to the old Iron curtain has more glamorous holiday villas. Until very recently even GDR citizens were not allowed to visit the border village of Sorge without a permit, and the village was kept for the exclusive use of loyal party apparatchiks. Both are now quiet walking and winter sports resorts surrounded by alpine-style meadows and dense forest.

Benneckenstein: This small former mining town keeps some light industry as well as being a winter sports and walking centre, with a lake and park; it makes a good accommodation base. One interesting piece of mining heritage is the annual finch singing contest (Finkenschlagen) held every Whitsuntide; finches like canaries (the Harzer Roller) were used as a warning of poor air quality in the Harz mines, and the annual contest is a relic of those days.

✳   ✳   ✳

WALK 18: THE UPPER BEHRE VALLEY
Benneckenstein to Ilfeld

The little River Behre forms one of several valleys which drain from the Harz mountains, this time southwards to Nordhausen, past villages and settlements conveniently served by the Harzquerbahn.

Distance:	12km (7$^{1}/_{2}$ miles)
Time:	4 hours
Public transport:	Harzquerbahn to Benneckenstein return from Ilfeld
Parking:	Park at Ilfeld Station and catch the train to the start of the walk
Map:	Wandern im Mittleren Harz
Refreshment facilities:	Sophienhof, Eisfelder Talmühle Station, Netzkater, Ilfeld

Route description: From Benneckenstein Station turn right into the centre of the town, turning right again at the crossroads towards Trautenstein, but taking the track almost opposite the parish church signed Sophienhof (red dot waymark). This soon crosses the little Rappbode stream and heads south-eastwards across open fields around the edge of the Pfeiferberg. Keep ahead past the edge of woods before the path descends over the Grauberg into the forest and the valley formed by the Krubergwasser stream, all these streams eventually joining the Bode and flowing to the north of the Harz.

The path bears left to join a track which climbs through forest over a low ridge to rejoin the railway line in the forest. The stream

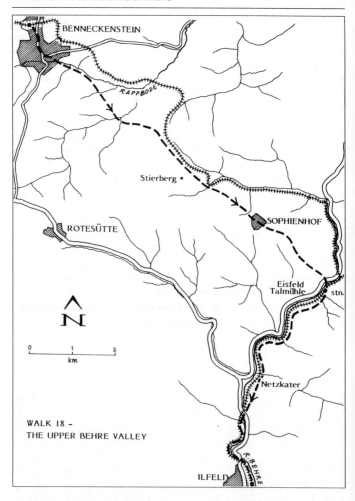

WALK 18 –
THE UPPER BEHRE VALLEY

at the far side of the railway is the Tiefenbach which is one of the tributaries of the River Behre which heads southwards towards Nordhausen. Follow the valley southwards until, as the railway line curves away to the right, the path with the red spot waymark climbs away from the railway and stream, and along a steeply wooded hillside before reaching a clearing and a crossroads at Sophienhof where there is an inn.

The route continues along a track still with the red waymarks and signed to Eisfelder Talmühle down Großer Schumannsstal to the busy main road at Eisefelder Talmühle in the narrow valley of the Behre.

Cross the railway immediately south of the station, but now take the yellow square waymarks and path which leads along the valley south-westwards following the railway and River Behre downhill along the valley bottom, with, if you've timed it right, some steam railway action as trains tackle the steep incline.

After 4km another road junction is reached; ahead is Netzkater, a small former mining settlement whose coal mine has been transformed into a fascinating museum. Should you decide to terminate the walk at this point, the station provides convenient return transport.

The final 3km to Ilfeld follows the track from the station from the main road and then continues with the orange square waymark down the valley past old paper mills before crossing the road with the railway at the level crossing, but soon recrossing the road to take a path along the edge of the woods into Ilfeld.

Points of interest:

Benneckenstein: see Walk 17

Eisfelder Talmühle: This hamlet and railway junction clearly takes its name from a valley noted for its icy conditions which once had a watermill on the Behre; it is now dominated by a nearby quarry and a busy railway junction where trains leave the Harzquerbahn on the mountainous link to the Selketalbahn to the east. At certain times of the day trains arrive here from Gernrode, Nordhausen and Wernigerode providing a complex series of interchanges as their locomotives are watered. The station has a cafe.

Netzkater: The Rabenstein Mine at Netzkater is a unique coal mine museum with a visible coal seam face and working underground railway. The mine is adjacent to the station and a visit can easily be combined with this walk.

Ilfeld: Ilfeld dates back to the early twelfth century when the

Thuringen nobility built a castle to guard the Behre valley. A monastery was established there in the sixteenth century, with a flourishing school which after 1945 was converted into a sanatorium, helping to establish Ilfeld as a holiday and sports centre for several large nationalised industries in the Communist era. Ilfeld enjoys a lovely setting; the old town centre with its half timbered houses and fine church has kept its character. There is an open-air forest swimming pool and some fine walks down the valley to Nordhausen or eastwards via the Poppenberg to the charming village of Neustadt.

* * *

WALK 19: OVER BIRKENMOOR
Stiege to Eisfelder Talmühle

This walk follows the steep and narrow pass which links the Selketalbahn and Harzquerbahn rail network, providing an opportunity to ride and walk one of the most dramatic parts of the Harz railway network.

Distance:	10km (6 miles)
Time:	3 hours
Public transport:	Harzquerbahn or Selketalbahn to Stiege, return from Eisfelder Talmühle
Parking:	Eisfelder Talmühle
Map:	Wandern im Mittleren Harz
Refreshment facilities:	Stiege, Birkenmoor, Eisfelder Talmühle station

Route description: From Stiege Station, take the track which begins immediately south of the station from the Birkenmoor road, waymarked with a green band on white. This heads due south, crossing open meadowland along the hillside above the railway with fine views before entering woods at Kaufung and descending to Birkenmoor halt on the railway. Cross the line.

Keep ahead on the track east of the station, heading almost due south into forest, still with the green-band-on-white waymark. The track climbs over Kronenberg before dipping into a shallow valley,

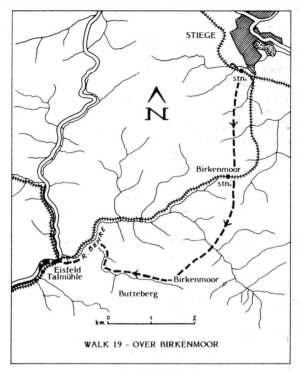

WALK 19 - OVER BIRKENMOOR

and bearing south-westwards. A steady climb now over the crown of a low ridge leads to Birkenmoor, a clearing in the forest with an inn.

A choice of ways, but perhaps the most pleasant descent is to head due west with the red spot waymarks into Großes Teichtal with its little ponds and into a narrow, steep gorge, fairly mountainous in appearance which descends to meet the main valley traversed by the railway, opposite the quarry.

Turn left along the track down into Eisfelder Talmühle.

To continue the walk to Ilfeld see Walk 18.

Points of interest:

Stiege: see Walk 23

Birkenmoor: The name literally means birch moor and reflects the kind of typical open birch woods and moorland which was probably even more prevalent than at present in the central Harz. The rail link between the Harzquerbahn and the Selketalbahn through what is a narrow, natural pass was not competed until 1905 and still forms a dramatic feature of the Harz railway network, through which ascending steam locomotives need to work especially hard to haul their loads up gradients of around 1 in 30.

Eisfelder Talmühle: see Walk 18

✳   ✳   ✳

WALK 20: SCHIERKE TO SORGE

A walk down the Elend valley which flows down from the Brocken massif, following the old East German border through forest rich in wildlife to the little resort of Sorge

Distance:	11km (7 miles)
Time:	$3^{1}/_{2}$ hours
Public transport:	Harzquer/Brockenbahn to Schierke, returning from Sorge
Parking:	Park at Drei Annen Hohne and catch train (or bus) to Schierke and return from Sorge to Drei Annen.
Map:	Wandern im Mittleren Harz
Refreshment facilities:	Schierke, Elend, Sorge

Route description: From Schierke Station follow the station drive down into the village, continuing past the church before turning left down the Elend road. Follow the green cross and blue triangle waymarks towards Elend which keep ahead where the main road crosses the bridge, continuing on a path on the far side of the river from the road down the Elend valley. Keep directly ahead where the road rejoins the path past Elendsburg into the centre of Elend.

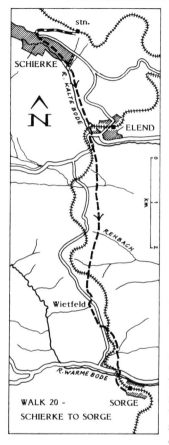

WALK 20 –
SCHIERKE TO SORGE

Leave along the Braunlage road, but where the road begins to climb and bears right, keep straight ahead along route 48G into the forest with the yellow dot way-mark signed Tanne. This crosses a track over the Speilbach and ascends Klausbruch.

After about 1½km there is a fork; take the right fork, signed 48F Sorge. This heads south-westwards crossing the Rehbach stream before climbing over the edge of another ridge not far from the railway, soon descending to cross the railway and meeting the road below at Wietfeld, where there's a forest lodge. At this point you are close to the former Iron Curtain, still indicated by a long narrow clearing in the forest above where once the fences ran and border guards patrolled.

The path follows the road for about 400m before taking a loop which crosses to the railway line before turning right, over the railway and south into a shallow valley, climbing over another shallow ridge before zigzagging down to cross the Warme Bode river and across the busy road junction into the village of Sorge.

The station and its nearby cafe lie up the hillside directly ahead.

Points of interest:

Schierke: see Walk 11

Elend: Elend derives its name from the period centuries ago when the monks used to make a pilgrimage from Ilsenburg in the Harz to

Rome. The district outside their monastery walls was regarded as *eli elend*. A characteristic of the landscape are the number of tors and like Schierke, it was a closed area during the Cold War. It contains the smallest wooden church in the Harz and is a noted winter sports centre.

Sorge: see Walk 17

✳   ✳   ✳

THE UNTERHARZ (Lower Harz)
Walks 21-30

The Unterharz or Lower Harz is, with certain exceptions such as the Bodetal, very much less well known than the Ober and Mittelharz. What the landscape lacks in grandeur, it makes up for in variety and richness. There are more deciduous woods, especially oak and beechwoods, and open farmland with glorious, herb-rich meadows and a variety of views.

Best centres are undoubtedly anywhere on the Selketalbahn, for example Alexisbad, Harzgerode, Güntersberge, Stiege or Hasselfelde, and perhaps Friedrichsbrunn, Treseburg, Elbingrode or Rübeland to reach the Bode valley. Stolberg in the south, though less central, would be a lovely place to stay.

Reichsbahn Hotel, Alexisbad

WALK 21: THE JOSEPHSKREUZ AND STOLBERG
Straßberg to Stolberg

An especially lovely and characteristic walk in the Unterharz, taking in two spectacular features - the Josephskreuz and the stunningly lovely half-timbered town of Stollberg.

Distance:	9km (6 miles)
Time:	3 hours
Public transport:	Selketalbahn to Straßberg; return by bus (K33 or K38) to Harzgerode or Alexisbad crossroads. Stolberg can also be reached by rail from the south via Berga-Kelbra for Sangerhausen or Nordhausen.
Parking:	Harzgerode and use train to Straßberg returning by bus as above.
Map:	Wandern im Mittleren Harz or KV Plan Auto & Wanderkarte (third edition) - slightly clearer.
Refreshment facilities:	Straßberg, Auerberg, Josephskreuz, Stolberg

Route description: From Straßberg Station walk back along the road parallel to the railway tracks to the crossroads, turning right towards the village centre, the Bergschänke Inn on the corner.

Unless you wish to explore this unspoiled Harz mining village by following the lane uphill, the route to Stolberg leaves along the lane westwards from the bottom crossroads, marked with a blue spot and also the blue St Andrews cross waymark.

At a junction where there's an old mine chauldron (truck), bear left with the blue spot waymark, the lane soon becoming a track out of the edge of the town, following the little Rodel valley past meadows and between woods. Keep ahead past a former children's holiday home, following the track as it curves south, and keeping ahead at a junction past old mine workings, and remains of a small pond. The track joins a broader track and enters forest.

At the next junction, still with the blue spot, turn left along a

STRASSBERG

Frankenteich

Auerberg

Josephskreuz
Tower

SIEBEN-WEG

WALK 21 –
THE JOSEPHSKREUZ
AND STOLBERG

ZECHENTAL

STOLBERG
(bus)

track in the woods which soon bears right through the forest up another valley before reaching an ascending dam which contains a lake, the Frankenteich. The path now veers off right to follow the shore of the lake of the Frankenteich, with attractive, reed fringed banks and open views.

Keep right with the path at the top of the lake to join another broader track for around 200m to where at a crossing, a path, marked by both red and blue spots, bears left by hedgerow and across open meadows, heading towards the wood ahead. Follow the waymarks in and around the field corner, the path going left around the headland and after about 100m, plunging to the right through the birch and beech-woods where it winds its way, well waymarked and clear on the ground, to the main road about 100m to the east of Auerberg crossroads where you'll find an inn, a car park and some open air snack stalls.

There is a choice of ways from here to the Josephskreuz. The nicest, if slightly steeper, is not along the main track which climbs due west, but a narrower path to the south marked with the yellow bar waymark, which goes deep into the forest, before swinging right and climbing steeply through woods to emerge at a splendid iron tower and viewing platform in the form of a cross - the Josephskreuz - and a viewpoint on the summit of Josephshöhe, with a cafe opposite.

Josephskreuz

The route back to Stolberg is about 60m back along the main track from Auerberg to where on the left and waymarked with a red cross, a narrow path plunges through the woods and shrubbery. Follow this steeply downhill to where it reaches another crossroads, Sieben Wege, where the easiest route is sharply to the left, still with the red cross, down the Zechental. This becomes a track though a steep wooded gorge by the Kleine Wilde stream, eventually broadening to a lane which enters the delightful town of Stolberg in its north-east corner. Give yourself plenty of time to explore this town. Buses leave either from the railway station at the bottom of the town or the bus stop in the Market above the town hall and information office by a small greengrocer's shop.

Points of interest:

Straßberg: This former mining village has converted part of the 600 year old Glasebach mine into a mining museum. At the time of writing, it is a village still emerging from a delightful time warp - with a village church with a timber tower shared between Catholics and Evangelicals, two welcoming inns, a post office, a saddler's, the mine rescue station, old fashioned shops and a sense of being well away from the rush of tourism and change. Evidence of mining will be seen along the walk, especially the ponds and lakes used to provide waterpower.

Josephskreuz: The striking iron cross which is used as a viewing point was originally of wood and first built in 1832/34 to the design of Karl Friedrich Schinkel. It was named after Josef von Stolberg, the count who had ordered its building. This original wooden cross burnt down after being struck by lightning.

In 1896 a replacement - this imposing 38m high, 125 tonne iron cross - was built by the Harz Club as a viewing tower. Two hundred steps take the visitor up to the top platform where there is a magnificent panorama of the southern Harz Mountains across to the Brocken in the west or as far Kyffhäuser and the Große Inselberg in the Thuringen Forest in the south, with the village of Schwenda in the foreground. The little Gasthof opposite provides refreshment with, on summer days, chairs and tables under the cross itself, and is highly commended for its home baked cakes.

Stolberg: Stolberg was the former residence of the powerful Counts of Stolberg whose castle on the hill overlooks the town. The counts whose wealth came from the rich mineral deposits in the area, minted their own gold and silver coins from the twelfth till the beginning of the nineteenth century. For a time weaving was also important to the town. The birthplace of Thomas Müntzer (1489-1525), contemporary of Martin Luther and leader of the peasants in the early sixteenth-century Peasant Wars, was burnt down some time ago, but in the market place there is a fine bronze sculpture which recalls the town's link with this folk hero and fighter for peasants' rights.

The town's former wealth is reflected in its architectural richness; streets which crowd for some considerable length along the valleys meet in the town centre, filled with half timbered houses of the sixteenth and seventeenth centuries, richly carved and decorated with carved sun rays, palm fronds, rosettes and many other details.

The town hall has no inside staircase to its upper stories which can only be reached by the adjoining steps to the church of St Martini. The town hall also contains 365 window panes, one for each day of the year and 52 windows to represent the appropriate number of weeks. The Museum in the Rittergasse is two stories high and one of the oldest houses in the town while the Heimatmuseum in the Thomas Müntzergasse, built in 1535, became the mint. It was at St Martini that Martin Luther preached against the Peasants' Revolt which was eventually put down with particular ferocity.

✳   ✳   ✳

WALK 22: THE UPPER SELKE VALLEY
Alexisbad to Straßberg

This walk from the fashionable resort of Alexisbad to the former mining village of Straßberg in the Selketal includes a visit to the lovely old town of Harzgerode.

Distance:	10km (6 miles)
Time:	3 hours
Public transport:	Selketalbahn to Alexisbad (or Harzgerode); return from Straßberg

Narrow gauge railways: Train arriving at Osterteich, near Gernrode

Narrow gauge railways: Brocken station
Early morning train at Eisfeleder Talmühle

Parking:	Alexisbad
Map:	KV Plan Auto & Wanderkarte (third edition)

Refreshment facilities: Alexisbad, Harzgerode, Straßberg

Route description: From Alexisbad Station walk along the main road eastward past the hotels, but look for the path on the right over a level crossing and footbridge over the River Selke. Turn left along the riverside, passing the small wooden chapel and small cave for another 150m to where a track to Harzgerode (waymarked with green spot) meets the riverside track. Turn right up here through the beech woods climbing steeply.

The track emerges on the outskirts of Harzgerode. Keep straight ahead along the road past houses and a church into the centre of Harzgerode, bearing left to the castle, station and market place.

To continue the walk, make your way down to the main Alexisbad road which runs below and to the south-west of the picturesque Market Place, and turn right in the direction back down to Alexisbad, passing a small lake on the left. Soon past the lake bear left along a lane, Silberhütte Straße, past houses. Where this ends, a track narrowing to a path continues, descending through fields alongside

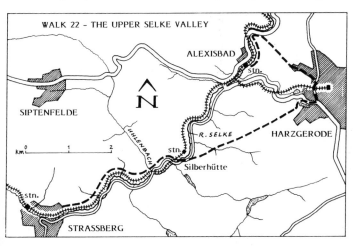

WALK 22 – THE UPPER SELKE VALLEY

ALEXISBAD

stn.

SIPTENFELDE

N

R. SELKE

HARZGERODE

km 0 1 2

UHLENBACH

stn.

Silberhütte

stn.

STRASSBERG

a hedge, and a grove of apple trees, dropping back into the Selke valley. Keep directly ahead to where the path enters Eisfeld Siedlung at the end of the path, joining a lane. Keep ahead in the same direction as the lane climbs uphill, continuing past the entrance to the old explosive works. Keep ahead to the centre of Silberhütte to the station by the woodyard. Follow the main road over the level crossing; the path, the Selkeweg, marked with a blue spot, joins the road and at the next crossing keeps ahead parallel to the railway alongside the track.

Where this track ends, keep ahead on the path alongside the railway and river waymarked with the blue spot, as they wind through the edge of woodland and into open countryside heading for Straßberg some 2km ahead. As you reach the crossroads, the station is straight ahead; the village centre and the Bergschänke inn are to your left.

Points of interest:

Alexisbad: This little resort was established by the Herzog (Duke) Alexius von Anhalt-Bernburg in 1816 as a spa to utilise the curative powers of its iron enriched mineral water, with a hotel and ornamental walks and viewpoints along the woods of the valley sides. The actual bath house named after Herzog Alexius had been built six years earlier. During the summer of 1812, 356 guests came by horse and carriage to Alexisbad to bathe in the waters and gamble in the newly opened casino. As its fame grew, such figures as the composer Carl Maria von Weber and the Danish writer Hans Christian Andersen found their way here to enjoy the area's beauty.

The resort expanded with the opening of the Selketal railway in 1891 resulting in the building of the handsome, pinnacled Alexisbad Hotel until recently owned and managed by East German Railways - the Reichsbahn - for its employees.

Several other big hotels were opened in the 1950s and 1960s during the communist era for party officials and senior managers of large state companies. These are now privatised, transforming the village into a Conference Centre and resort with an excellent choice of reasonably priced quality accommodation, strategically situated on the railway line where tracks separate for Hasselrode and Harzgerode, the simultaneous departure of the two steam hauled trains at the graded junction each day is a unique event which now attracts steam buffs from all over Europe.

Harzgerode: In 970 Otto III granted the monastery of Thanksmarsfelde market rights and the right to mint their own coins in Harzgerode. By the thirteenth century, the town's poverty-stricken inhabitants found themselves having to pay tithes both to the abbots and their aristocratic overlords. Not surprisingly the town became a mustering point in the Lower Harz and Thuringia for supporters of the peasant cause in the sixteenth-century Peasant War. It was also a centre of the mining industry where silver, copper, iron, sulphur and vitriol was mined, silver being particularly important, and certain rights and privileges (Bergfreiheiten) were granted to the miners as a result by the emperor.

There is a particularly fine Town Hall. On the eastern side of the Market Place stands the church of St Marien. This dates from 1383, a miners' church with wooden interior and appropriate detail of mining techniques. The three storey castle with its round tower has a museum with many interesting documents about mining history as well as details of historic and pre-historic settlements in the area. The parquet floor of the banqueting hall is made of various types of wood to be found in the Harz forests.

Silberhütte: This small mining settlement takes its name from the silver and lead mines which once existed in the area. In more recent years it was the site of a large factory producing explosives for use in the mining industry. It is now a fraction of its size and facing closure. Its tall factory chimney, for many years a notable landmark in Selketal is due to be demolished. Silberhütte has a delightful period station in the centre of a woodyard. Sadly most of the complex of rail sidings to the woodyard and the explosive works are no longer used.

Straßberg: see Walk 21

WALK 23: AROUND HASSELFELDE AND STIEGE
Hasselfelde to Güntersberge

Between the watershed of the rivers Hassel and Selke are open fields and herb rich meadows so characteristic of the Unterharz. N.B. Recent changes in the rail timetable may make this walk easier to complete in the reverse direction.

Distance:	13km (8 miles)
Time:	4 hours
Public transport:	Selketalbahn to Hasselfelde and return from Güntersberge. Bus K39 provides a later service to Harzgerode, Alexisbad crossroads and Quedlinburg.
Parking:	Güntersberge then take the train to Hasselfelde.
Map:	Wandern im Mittleren Harz or KV Plan Auto & Wanderkarte (third edition)
Refreshment facilities:	Hasselfelde, Stiege, Güntersberge

Route description: From Hasselfelde Station walk up the hill to the town centre, turning right along the main street past the old town hall and church in the centre. Past the church, turn left downhill, but take the first turning right, going left again on a residential road immediately behind the church which ends in a track between allotments (waymarked with a red square) to the Rabensfels. Follow the track eastwards past fields to the Rabenfels (Ravens Rock) from where it bears right on a narrow track below a hedge, with good views towards Stiege with its distinctive and space-age watertower. Keep ahead on the path as it curves towards the woods ahead. The path now enters woods (used for motor cycle trails so be careful at weekends) and continues along a hedge; keep right at a junction with the red square waymarks, down to the main road at the youth hostel.

Still with the red square waymarks, follow the track immediately to the left which leads past the entrance to the youth hostel, and its

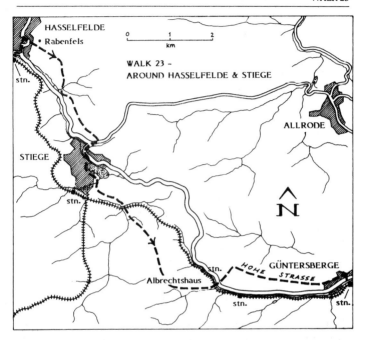

adjacent camp site, beyond which it turns sharp right, again following a hedge and crossing fields with fine views across to Stiege with its modernistic water tower. The path descends to join a track and a busy road just before a junction. Turn right, going straight ahead at the junction to walk directly ahead into the little lakeside resort of Stiege with its choice of inns and cafes.

Take the path alongside the boating and swimming lake, keeping around the shores of the lake along a road to its far side to where just before a second lake closer to the railway, a path signed to Albrechtshaus (red triangle) bears left parallel to the little river Hassel and the railway with the wooded Mühlberg hill to the left.

Keep ahead on the red triangle route past open fields which after a little less than 1km crosses the railway and ascends the other side. Keep on the main track, now crossing beautiful open meadows rich in wild flowers, with fine open views on all sides. After a little more

117

than 1km, the path enters forest and gradually descends into another valley formed by the Stiegerbach. Turn left here, following the waymarks to bear left again through woods into Albrechtshaus, a hamlet linked to a large sanatorium, and noted for its lovely little wooden church which you pass on the route.

A railway station (and bus terminus) here will enable you to cut the walk short at this point. Otherwise bear right to where a level crossing and bridge over the Selke leads up to the main road. Here the path marked with both a yellow spot and a green square waymark leads (signed Güntersberge and Allrode) steeply uphill to a broad crossing track, the Hohe Straße, marked with the green square waymark.

Turn right here for an easy walk of around 2¹/₂km at first through forest but later through open fields along a low ridge before entering the outskirts of Güntersberge, with its boating lake, a former millpond, on the right. The railway station (with refreshment room) is at the far end of the village below the Schwarzer Bär (Black Bear) inn. There is also a useful bus service down the valley.

Points of interest:

Hasselfelde: Another former mining town dominated by characteristic clapboard architecture, Hasselfelde has a long main street with an old town hall, charming turn of century post office in decorated style, fine parish church and some quiet and sleepy back ways - the kind of place that people go through rather than stay very long in. There is a ruined castle to the north of the town and about 4km to the north the huge Rappbode Reservoir.

Stiege: Stiege was first recorded as a settlement as early as 1442. The old castle of the same name was originally a defensive fortification, but then was used as a hunting castle and later for municipal offices and the local judiciary. The town's name came from the word "Stieg", the name for a narrow path or road which led over the mountains; the village lay on a medieval trade route. Ores were mined and smelted here for many years to be followed by the brewing of beer and the production of Harz cheese. It is now a small but attractive summer resort, its main attraction being the surrounding countryside and its twin lakes, popular for boating and swimming.

Wooden church, Albrechtshaus

Güntersberge: Güntersberge is a small town in the Harz; occupying a sheltered position in the Selke valley on the edge of the forest. This former mining settlement has developed into a particularly attractive summer resort. The lake created when the River Selke was dammed to provide power for a mill lake now provides an attractive boating and swimming facility with lido.

* * *

28/10/10 **WALK 24: ALEXISBAD TO GERNRODE VIA THE KLIPPENWEG**

Spectacular scenery on the first part of this walk along the Klippenweg, followed by the remarkable industrial revolution settlement of Mägdesprung, provides a prelude to exploring the old Harz town of Gernrode.

Distance:	15km (9 miles)
Time:	4 hours
Public transport:	Selketalbahn to Alexisbad and from Gernrode. Gernrode is on the standard gauge branch railway from Quedlinburg and Aschersleben.
Parking:	Gernrode and catch the train to Alexisbad.
Map:	KV Plan Auto & Wanderkarte (third edition)
Refreshment facilities:	Alexisbad, Mägdesprung, Sternhaus, Gernrode

Route description: From Alexisbad Station walk back down the main road past the hotels, crossing to the level crossing and footbridge over the railway. Turn left along the path along the River Selke, past the little chapel and a cave, emerging on the main road after about 1km near Klostermühle.

Keep on the same side of the road to where the path continues - the Klippenweg - at first parallel with the railway but gradually climbing the hillside through woods. The path soon climbs away from the valley, reaching and going through an intriguing tunnel

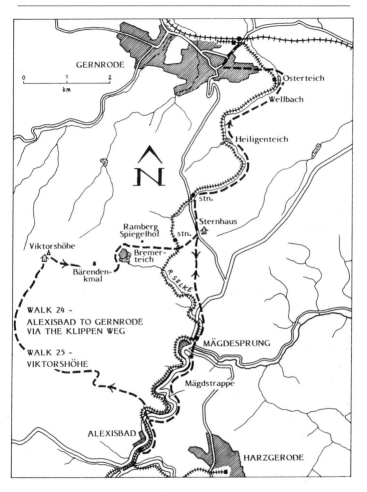

GERNRODE

Osterteich

Wellbach

Heiligenteich

stn.

Sternhaus

Ramberg
Spiegelhof   stn.

Viktorshöhe   Bremer-
teich

Bärenden-
kmal

R. SELKE

WALK 24 -
ALEXISBAD TO GERNRODE
VIA THE KLIPPEN WEG

MÄGDESPRUNG

WALK 25 -
VIKTORSHÖHE

Mägdstrappe

ALEXISBAD

HARZGERODE

built by the Pioneers - communist version of Boy Scouts - presumably as an engineering exercise, which carries the path through a sandstone crag. Keep the same direction through beautiful oak woods as the path drops across a shallow valley with a crossing track to ascend through scrub back to the cliff, soon passing a newly

Mägdesprüng - panorama view across Selketal

restored summer house and a spectacular viewpoint.

Continue the same way following signs to the Mägdstrappe, an intriguing iron pillar and magnificent viewpoint, still in superb oak woods; a weather worn bench enables the walker to enjoy a superb view into the deep, thickly wooded and winding gorge of the Selke below. Follow the narrow path as it zigzags down the steep hillside to emerge at the road junction south of the old ornamental iron manufacturing village of Mägdesprung (5km - trains from here back to Alexisbad).

The footpath continues along a route waymarked with a red spot parallel and to the south side of the railway. This follows a stream up the main road; cross and almost opposite continue along the track through the forest which leads up to Sternhaus, a large inn at the crossroads.

The path continues for a little less than 1km alongside the main road almost due north to Sternhaus Haferfeld Station - a tiny halt by an open crossing with little more than a station sign to announce that trains stop.

Take the track on the right just before the crossing which curves down through the woods, going below the railway line and past a small lake, the Heiligenteich. The track continues through the woods until it enters a small lido, Osterteich at a gate; unless you decide to catch a train at Osterteich Station to the left, keep ahead through and below the lido where you turn left along the track, then left back across a level crossing and into the centre of Gernrode down a long street; turn right in the town centre down to Gernrode's twin stations, standard and narrow gauge, for return transport. There is a buffet in the main line station.

Points of interest:

Mägdstrappe: The iron post marks the place where, according to legend, a young female giant wanted to visit her friend across the Selke gorge. She hesitated when she saw what a distance she would have to leap. A passing farmer in his cart mocked the young giantess, whereupon she picked him up in her skirts, cart and all, and leapt safely across with him to the other side.

Mägdesprung: The legend gave the name to the village at the crossroads below the Mägdstrappe which divides the upper and lower Selketal.

The village is rich in largely undiscovered industrial archaeology and historic interest. An ironworks was established by one of the Anhalt princes here in 1646 to smelt locally produced ores with ample supplies of timber for fuel. Many of the buildings and works including the neo-classical main buildings with a clock tower date from the eighteenth century. The works which are still open specialised in ornamental cast iron since 1821, including some striking substantial works of art such as an enormous stag with branching antlers attacked by hounds which decorates the village green and the stag outside the hotel Harzquell at Alexisbad. Note the cast iron statue to the Prince of Anhalt.

The railway station, a passing loop on the Selketalbahn, has a delightful refreshment room with a projecting window giving a fine view of the railway.

Gernrode: In 959, the Margrave Gero gave a convent church on land at the edge of the Harz mountains in what is now Gernrode to his widowed daughter-in-law, Hathiu, who was appointed its first abbess. In time the foundation became so rich and powerful, it owned vast areas of land and became one of the four richest in Germany. Only the church of St Cyriakus remains of the original buildings and it is one of the finest Romanesque sacred buildings in the region.

The small town is also noted for its fine town hall and pleasant, if neglected suburbs. Its handsome old railway station is the northern interchange point with main line services onto the Selketalbahn.

✳   ✳   ✳

WALK 25: VIKTORSHÖHE
Alexisbad to Sternhaus Ramberg or Mägdesprung

An exhilarating forest walk along tracks to Viktorshöhe, one of the highest points in the Unterharz, returning into the Selketal via Mägdesprung

Distance:	16km (10 miles) or 13km (8m) if terminated at Sternhaus Ramberg
Time:	4 or 5 hours
Public transport:	Selketalbahn to Alexisbad and from Mägdesprung.
Parking:	Alexisbad and return by train.
Map:	KV Plan Auto & Wanderkarte (third edition). Route Map p121
Refreshment facilities:	Alexisbad; Viktorshöhe, Mägdesprung (station)

Route description: From Alexisbad Station walk back down the main road past the hotels, crossing to the level crossing and footbridge over the railway. Turn left along the path along the River Selke, past the little chapel and cave, emerging on the main road after about 1km near Klostermühle.

Cross the road, and take the forest track alongside the former hostel signed to Viktorshöhe (green spot waymark), soon crossing the railway line.

The track ascends a narrow valley, ascending and curving northwards through mainly tall coniferous woods - commercial woodlands. At a junction keep left with the green spot waymark ascending a steep valley for 4kms gradually curving northwards above the Friedrichstalbach valley. The track finally emerges at a clearing past a pool, the Erichburger Teich and a crossroads; turn right here, for about 500m before turning left at the next junction to follow the yellow spot waymarks, keeping ahead and up hill to Viktorshöhe (582m), the highest point of the Ramsberg ridge with a viewpoint in the centre of the forest where there is an inn. Huge blocks of granite nearby are known as the Teufelsmühle - the Devil's millstones.

Viktorshöhe is at a crossroads of tracks, including paths down to Friedrichsbrunn. To return into the Selketal, leave by the track leading south-eastwards signed Bremer Teich and Sternhaus. Keep straight ahead at a crossroads, the track quickly losing height through the woods.

Look out for the Bärendenkmal, a stone memorial at the side of the track to your left.

Turn left at the next junction to the Bremer Teich, a forest swimming pool and holiday camp, but at the next junction turn right signed for Sternhaus, past a forester's house known as Spiegelhof, and descend through thick forest to the railway line.

Sternhaus Ramberg Station, a tiny wayside halt, basically a signboard and a shelter, is about 200m on the left along the track by the railway; if you are continuing to Mägdesprung, keep straight ahead for a further 500m to Sternhaus, an inn and car park strategically situated by the crossroads.

The track to Mägdesprung lies along the track due south marked with a red spot waymark; follow this for almost 2km to where it meets the main road; the path crosses the road to follow the stream emerging in the centre of Mägdesprung close by the railway station.

Points of interest:

Bärendenkmal: The last wild bear in the forests of Sachsen-Anhalt and probably the entire Harz region was killed in the late seventeenth century. This stone marks the place where the actual slaughter occurred, and is a reminder of man's on-going responsibility for the natural world so easily destroyed by thoughtless action.
Mägdesprung: see Walk 24

＊　　＊　　＊

WALK 26: BODETAL
Thale to Treseburg

A famous and popular walk through the magnificent Bode Valley Nature Reserve

Distance:	10km (6 miles)
Time:	3 hours, plus time to explore the Hexentanzplatz and/or the Roßtrappe. This can easily be made into a circular walk back to Thale via the Rennsteig - an additional 8km (5 miles).

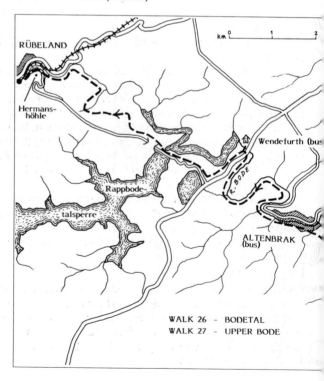

Public transport:	Thale is served by regular trains from Blankenburg, Quedlinburg and Wernigerode. There are bus services from Treseburg back to Thale (K18 and H272) and to Blankenburg (H263). There is also a limited service direct to and from Thale from Harzgerode and Alexisbad via Allrode.
Parking:	Thale
Map:	KV Plan Auto & Wanderkarte (third edition)
Refreshment facilities:	Thale, Jungfernbrücke, Tresburg

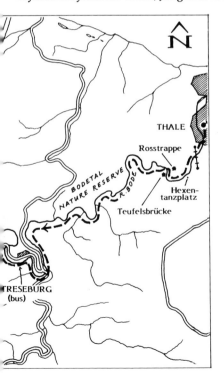

Route description: From Thale Station entrance cross to the park, leaving by the top right hand corner, following the road down to the bridge and the cable-car station to the Hexentanzplatz, with the chairlift to the Roßtrappe nearby.

Allow time either to take the cable-car or walk to and from the Hexantanzplatz to enjoy spectacular views along the Bode valley.

The main path up the valley (blue triangle) starts at the cable-car station and is a broad, busy track under the cables and along the narrow gorge, soon reaching the Jungfernbrücke (inn) from where there are steps up to the Hexentanzplatz, and winding its way past the Goethe plaque and the steps leading up to the Roßtrappe to the Teufelsbrücke - Devil's Bridge.

From here the path becomes a narrow, stony way, climbing steeply up the cliffside with the occasional viewpoint down into the fierce gorge of the Bode or up to the pinnacles of the Roßtrappe crags above. This section of the valley is known as the Bodekessel (normally "Kessel" is a geographical term for a basin shaped valley), but here the water literally seems to froth and boil through the narrow gorge.

The path is easy to follow, and after climbing up the side of the crag, descends to river level and broadens to become an easy, level track, through glorious deciduous woods, rich in wild flowers, all of it a Nature reserve. Continue along the serpentine valley, the path occasionally moving away from the river, at times following the river edge.

At one steep dip close by a small wayside shelter (7km) a broader track comes in from the left. Ignore it. The way is to the right, ascending and curving back towards the river, before eventually curving round into a long loop and joining the main road by the bridge at Treseburg. Buses for Thale and Blankenburg leave from the bus station, reached from the end of the Bodetal path by turning right and crossing over the bridge.

This walk can be extended using Walk 28 as far as Allrode or Walk 27 as far as Altenbrak for return transport. Alternatively to make a circular walk, take the path waymarked with a red spot signed to Thale which leaves from the southern end of the village and climbs steeply through the forest up the Hagensdornberg (viewpoint) before turning right along a forest track and heading due east along further tracks along the ridge. Keep with the red spot waymark as the path turns north-eastwards to emerge eventually at the Hexentanzplatz with a choice of paths or even cable-car back to Thale town centre.

Points of interest:

Thale: Part tourist town part industrial centre with a large steel works, Thale is a natural gateway for the exploration of the Bode valley with the Hexentanzplatz and Roßtrappe close by. The town has gardens, mineral springs and a good choice of accommodation and refreshment facilities.

The Hexentanzplatz: The Hexentanzplatz can be reached by cable railway in four minutes or climbed by stepped path from the valley bottom. Apart from unforgettable views from the cable-car ride or foot ascent climb along the length of the Bodetal, and from the Hexantanzplatz crags themselves, there are many other things worth seeing. The Walpurgis Hall was built there as a museum in 1901 and houses a series of exhibitions, including a permanent collection of pictures which were inspired by the Walpurgisnacht scenes in Goethe's *Faust*. There is also a sacrificial stone dating from pre-historic times. Nearby is the open-air theatre founded in 1903, a superb setting for 1400 spectators to watch a variety of theatrical performances from May to September. There is also a zoo with over 400 native species.

Archaeological finds on the Roßtrappe and the Hexentanzplatz indicate that both areas were the centre for ritual sacrifices in prehistoric times.

Roßtrappe: Opposite the Hexentanzplatz is a 403m high granite cliff known as the Roßtrappe after a legend about a lovely Princess Brunhilde, pursued by the Knight Bodo on his giant steed. When she reached this deep gorge, the princess spurred her horse and leapt across. To this day there is an impression of what looks likes a horse's hoof on the stone on the cliff top.

As Bodo in turn tried to follow her, his horse missed its footing and he plunged down to his death in the river - ever since called after him. In addition, as a further punishment, he was turned into a massive ugly hound who was forever compelled to guard the princess's crown which fell into the River Bode as she was being pursued.

There is a footpath up to the Roßtrappe and also a chairlift to enjoy magnificent views into the Bode valley and as far out into the Harz foreland as Halberstadt and Quedlinburg.

Bodetal Nature Reserve: Almost the entire Bode valley is a Nature Reserve, not only for its splendid geological formation, but superb beechwoods rich in wild flowers in the spring months - especially for orchids. The area has been intensively visited by tourists since the eighteenth century.

Treseburg: Treseburg takes its name from a medieval castle perched on a bend above the river, but the modern village owes everything to catering for the thousands of visitors who come to experience the remarkable natural beauty of the Bodetal.

*   *   *

WALK 27: UPPER BODE
Treseburg to Rübeland

A walk to take in the top end of the Bode Valley including the celebrated Rappbode Reservoir with its 405m long and 106m high dam.

Distance:	16km (10 miles)
Time:	5 hours
Public transport:	Bus H263 from Blankenburg, H272 from Wernigerode or Rübeland, K18 from Thale. Return by rail or bus from Rübeland.
Parking:	Blankenburg, then return by train or bus.
Map:	Wandern im Mittleren Harz or KV Plan Auto & Wanderkarte (third edition) . Route Map p126/127
Refreshment facilities:	Treseburg, Altenbrak, Wendefurth, Rübeland

Route description: From Treseburg bus station follow the main road across the bridge over the River Bode, turning immediately right along a picturesque riverside track (blue and green triangle waymarks) along the river gorge behind the village. Follow this track as it winds to the left below a crag known as the Wildstein, through the Bode gorge. The path joins the road for a short way as the river loops to the north before once again leaving along the riverside past the Falkenklippe - the Falcon Crags. Keep ahead over another forested knoll into the road which leads into Altenbrak.

Unless you are going to explore the centre of this attractive village, do not cross the bridge, but continue along the path along the south side of the river, still with the blue triangle waymark. This path follows the wooded gorge of the River Bode in a long, serpentine loop eventually reaching the main Blankenburg-Hasselfelde road at Wendefurth, a small resort where there's an inn and a car park.

From here the blue diamond route follows the lane, before bearing right across a corner, and keeping right to follow the lane over the Rappbode Reservoir dam. Keep ahead parallel to the lane for another kilometre before following a forest track still with the blue triangle, which curves northwards over the Harmsberg and above Neumerk, turning left above the valley and following the curve of the hillside before meeting the lane which descends steeply into Rübeland. Passing the entrance to the Baumannshöhle and the Hermannshöhle with the railway station on the left.

Points of interest:

Treseburg: see Walk 26

Altenbrak: An attractive village and small resort perched high above the River Bode. There are some interesting houses as well as a swimming pool. The Harz yodelling contest - another typical Harz custom - is held here each year.

The Rappbode Reservoir and Dam: This 450m long, 106m high dam provides a spectacular viewpoint across the reservoir and into the Bode Valley. The reservoir contains almost 110 million cubic metres of water and provides drinking water for the industrial conurbations of Halle and Magdeburg.

Rübeland: The Rübeland lies in an area of carboniferous limestone, and for this reason there are several major quarries. There are also numerous natural caves, the finest being the Baumannshöhle and the Hermannshöhle, both now popular and well-lit show caves.

The Baumannshöhle was discovered in 1536 in a tragic way by a local miner called Baumann. Walking home after a terrible storm, he noticed a huge split in the rocks which he had not seen previously. With the help of his miner's lamp he decided to explore the ravine, crawling through it with difficulty on hands and knees to discover an enormous cave system. Unfortunately he got totally lost as his lamp went out, and it took him three days and nights to find his way out again. When he did so, he was in a desperately exhausted and weakened state. Nevertheless he was able to describe in some detail the beauty of the superb formations he had seen, but sadly died shortly afterwards, not recovering from his ordeal. The largest cave in the Baumannshöhle is a vast 40m high by 60m long with an imposing arch and a crystal clear lake. Other features are the so-called Palm Grotto and the Gorge of the Turtles. The deepest part of the cave is 68m.

The Hermannshöhle was discovered in 1866 and the visitor has 1,200m of underground paths to explore, leading to beautiful grottoes and caves such as the Bear' Cemetery with the spectacular Crystal Cave as the climax.

Outside the caves on the heights of the Kleef, there is a temple-style viewing pavilion dating from 1892.

✳   ✳   ✳

WALK 28: THE LUPPBODE AND RABENTAL
Treseburg to Allrode or Friedrichsbrunn

Less well known than its busier neighbour, the Luppbode, a tributary valley of the Bode has woodland of great beauty. Paths link either to the village of Allrode or to the forset resort of Friedrichsbrunn.

Distance:	12km (7 miles)
Time:	3$^{1}/_{2}$ hours
Public transport:	Buses H263, H272, K18, to Treseburg: K18, K318 back to Thale.
Parking:	In Friedrichsbrunn and catch K18 to Treseburg

| *Map:* | Wandern im Mittleren Harz or KV Plan |
| | Auto & Wanderkarte (third edition) |

Refreshment facilities: Treseburg, Allrode, Friedrichsbrunn

Route description: From Treseburg bus station walk southwards past the last inn of the village, taking the path immediately to the left which crosses a footbridge (yellow square or red bar on white waymark) which winds its way behind gardens before becoming a narrow track, parallel to the road, winding up the Luppbode valley. You soon cross another footbridge and pass a car park and picnic area. Cross the track ahead, keeping in the same direction up the valley along a path which narrows.

Where the parallel road swings away to your left you reach a steep and narrow crossing valley. Follow the path into this valley before bearing right along a path which descends to a footbridge before ascending and joining a track on the other side - waymarked to Allrode.

Turn left, climbing steadily up the Rabental, going deep into the forest. After about 1km the track forks; follow the waymarks (red band or yellow spot) to the right, crossing the brow of the hill into

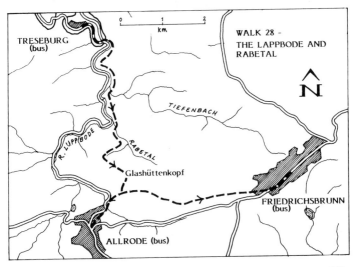

an area of young forest. Look for the waymarked path (red band) which turns right along a narrow path past larch trees before plunging steeply downhill through beech woods to meet a tarmac forest track below.

If you decide to go to the village of Allrode (buses to Güntersberge, Alexisbad crossroads or back to Treseburg) turn right to the main road. From here turn left into Allrode. The bus stops are beside the inn in the village centre.

But if you are completing the walk to Friedrichsbrunn, turn left at the forest track, now following a green St Andrews cross waymark. Where the track bears left, the green cross route goes straight through the forest, along the side of the valley of Brumshals. Follow this path as it contours its way through the forest, following the edge of the forest and parallel to the road westwards before descending into the outskirts of Friedrichsbrunn.

Points of interest:

Treseburg: see walk 26

Luppbode Valley: Though nothing like as famous as the main Bode valley, this is a valley of great beauty dominated by fine beechwoods. Look out for the remains of old mine workings and a small adit or mine entrance like a cave along the footpath about 2km south of Treseburg.

Allrode: A small, typical quiet Unterharz village lying in a large forest clearing of open farmland, and well off the main tourist trails, with a quiet main street, an inn, a small supermarket and some old farmhouses built in traditional style.

Friedrichsbrunn: The highest resort in the Unterharz, lying between 560m and 587m above sea level. It was founded in 1774/75 by Russian colonists who worked as woodcutters, stone cutters and charcoal burners. In 1870 the villagers started to export spruce trees for Christmas trees to places as far away as Berlin and Hamburg, a trade that continues. It is also a health spa in the forest following the discovery of a pure spring well in 1770, the Friedrichsbrunn, which gave the town its name. Now a centre for winter sports, it's also a popular walking and outdoor centre, with direct bus services from the conurbations of Magdeburg and Halle.

✻   ✻   ✻

WALK 29: THE KÖNIGSBURG AND RÜBELAND
Königshütte circular

A circular walk in the predominantly limestone country of Rübeland in the Upper Bode valley.

Distance:	16km (10 miles)
Time:	5 hours
Public transport:	Trains from Blankenburg (connections from Wernigerode) to Königshütte and return; the walk can be terminated at Rübeland (8km), or turned into a 8km circular walk by returning via Pappenberg to Königshütte from the reservoir dam.
Parking:	Königshütte
Map:	Wandern im Mittleren Harz
Refreshment facilities:	Königshütte, Rübeland

Route description: From Königshütte Station head southwards through the village on the road towards Tanne, following the route signed Rübeland, blue triangle waymark, which turns left to cross the river just south of the village and close to the ruins of the Königsburg Castle on the right, before following a forest track along the southern bank of the Überleitungsperre in the upper Bode valley.

Continue for about 4km to the reservoir dam; the route continues along a broad track up the narrow Bode Valley crossing a narrow ravine before joining a minor road which leads into Rübeland.

The return to Königshütte is the route marked by a yellow St Andrews cross route or white-fir-tree-on-red-ground waymarks - the latter indicating a forest trail with explanatory notices showing types of trees. From Rübeland, this leaves along the steeply winding road past the Hermannshöhle, climbing out of Rübeland towards Altenbrak. Follow the hairpin bend and at the next bend, bear off right along a forest track with the fir tree and yellow cross waymarks.

This track climbs a steep forested gorge which eventually joins a tarmac lane. Keep with the forest trail, the white and red fir tree (29G), turning left along a broad track which follows the ridge for another 2km, before the waymarks indicate a track down a steep

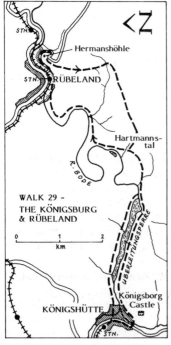

WALK 29 -
THE KÖNIGSBURG
& RÜBELAND

narrow gorge to the right - Hartmannstal - which rejoins the track up the Bodetal from Königshütte (blue triangle).

Turn left along the track and return to the dam, this time taking the path across the dam. At the far side go a short way up the hill before turning left with the blue St Andrews cross waymark along a track which follows the north bank of the reservoir through forest. Keep ahead past the Papenberg and across the Papenbach, going out of the forest and ahead into the outskirts of Königshütte.

Points of interest:

Rübeland: see Walk 27

The Rübeland Railway: The 24km long standard gauge Rübelandbahn was primarily built to serve the huge limestone quarries of the Upper Bode valley. It was largely rebuilt and electrified in the 1960s to demonstrate the ability of efficient modern electric locomotives to cope with gradients of up to 60% without the need of rack systems. Even so, heavy freight trains have to have locomotives at either end to get trains around the railway's steep curves up murderous gradients and to restrain descending loads of limestone.

Königshütte: This is a small township which takes its name from the Königsburg, a ruined hunting lodge built in the eleventh century by King Heinrich III of Saxony.

The Überleitungstalsperre: The reservoir passed on this walk is literally a connecting reservoir fed by the Warme and Kalte Bode rivers and the Mandelholz Reservoir, and linked to the massive Rappbode Reservoir to the south (Walk 27).

✳ ✳ ✳

WALK 30: TO QUEDLINBURG
Gernrode to Quedlinburg

A walk chosen not so much for its intrinsic scenic qualities as a fitting way to approach, through the Harz foreland, one of Europe's most beautiful medieval towns; give yourself plenty of time to discover this World Heritage Site.

Distance:	11km (7 miles)
Time:	3$^{1}/_{2}$ hours
Public transport:	Gernrode (terminus of the Selketalbahn) and Quedlinburg are linked by the standard gauge branch railway to Aschersleben. Bus K39 also provides a direct link from Harzgerode and Alexisbad to Gernrode and Quedlinburg. 2km can be saved by alighting from the train at Bad Suderode Station.
Parking:	Near Gernrode Station and return by train.
Map:	KV Plan Auto & Wanderkarte (third edition)

Refreshment facilities: Gernrode, Quedlinburg

Route description: From Gernrode Station turn right outside the station entrance by the level crossing, and walk towards the town centre, bearing right along the Bad Suderode road 2km to Bad Suderode Station, bear right along the lane past Bad Suderode Station. This road soon becomes a quiet farm road, well signed and marked with a red spot waymark.

Where the track turns left, keep straight ahead due north along a path across open fields alongside a ditch which soon joins the Quarmbach stream. Keep alongside the fields until the path and stream meet the main road near Quarmbeck station. Cross, continuing alongside the stream heading northwards for another 2$^{1}/_{2}$km before reaching and crossing the main Blankenburg railway line; keep ahead, the path now reaching the outskirts of Quedlinburg, crossing the River Bode.

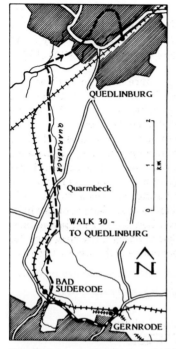

QUEDLINBURG

QUARMBACK

Quarmbeck

WALK 30 –
TO QUEDLINBURG

BAD
SUDERODE

GERNRODE

Turn right into Brühlstraße, soon going into and directly across Brühl Park, emerging at the north-east corner, bearing right then first left to Bilnstraße and ahead into the main Ottostraße. Turn left and then along a choice of narrow streets on the right which lead past the castle and the Market Place in the town centre.

The bus and rail stations are to the eastern side of the town.

Points of interest:

Gernrode: see Walk 24

Quarmbeck: The fields around Quedlinburg are famous for the production of flower seeds in both glasshouses and in the open fields making this area a blaze of colour in spring and in early summer, earning Quedlinburg its title "Blumenstadt am Harz".

Quedlinburg: Probably founded in the fifth century, Quedlinburg was named after a Thuringian aristocrat called Quitilo who built the first fortification on the Burgberg. The town grew after its tenth century religious foundation was granted market rights, plus the right to mint its own coins and erect custom controls; it flourished to such a degree that it became a member of the Hanseatic League, and though it was later to be overtaken in importance by rivals, its prosperity largely continued.

The poet and philosopher Gottfried Klopstock (1724-1803) lived here and his home is now a museum; another celebrity was Germany's first woman doctor Dorothea Erxleben (1715-62).

The town contains around 1,000 half-timbered houses; 330 of them are listed buildings, a wealth of late Gothic (fifteenth century), sixteenth-, seventeenth- and eighteenth-century buildings of outstanding quality, including the two-storied Ständebau which is Quedlingburg's oldest half-timbered house, dating from the fourteenth century, and though restored one of Germany's and Europe's oldest houses in that style. It is now a museum of half-timbering.

Because of its architectural importance, the town was recently granted World Heritage status by UNESCO. A walk through the town's narrow streets is an unforgettable experience, despite the amount of restoration work that still has to be done.

The green-creeper covered town hall in the extensive Market Place dates from the early fourteenth century and has a Renaissance doorway of 1616. Nearby the symbolic figure of Roland guards the town's civil liberties and each side of the town hall is flanked by some superb examples of half-timbering. The ascent to the castle from the old town goes by the Finkenherd, a collection of fine half-timbered buildings. This is the place where Henry I, the Saxon King, so the story goes, was offered the German crown. The view from the castle ramparts offers a splendid panorama of the town's mosaic of tiled roofs and steeples.

✳   ✳   ✳

PART THREE
USEFUL WORDS AND PHRASES

For non-German speaking ramblers we have compiled a brief list of some of the common words and phrases you're likely to meet or need in the Harz area. For those with some knowledge of German, you will find that there are certain words and phrases included which are particularly characteristic for this region.

On the Route

Path	der Pfad	Map	die Landkarte
Road	die Straße/Gaße	River	der Fluß
Forest path	der Waldweg	Lake	der See
Fir tree	die Fichte	Bridge	die Brücke
Pine tree	die Tanne	Half-timbered	
Meadow	die Wiese	house	das Fachwerkhaus
Boundary/border	die Grenze	Local museum	das Heimatmuseum

Monastery	das Stift	Do you speak	Sprechen Sie
Town hall	das Rathaus	English?	Englisch?
Tower	der Turm, der	I don't under-	
	Aussichtsturm	stand	Ich verstehe nicht
Shelter hut	die Schutzhütte	Please speak	Bitte, sprechen Sie
Shooting hut/		more slowly	noch langsamer
platform	die Jagdkanzel	I am lost	Ich habe mich
Clearing on the			verirrt
mountain	die Schneise	Can you help	Können Sie mir
Medicinal plants	die Heilpflanzen	me?	helfen?
Foxglove	der Fingerhut	How far is it to...?	Wie weit ist es von
Butterfly	der Schmetterling/		hier nach...?
	Falter	Is this the way	Ist das der weg
		to...?	nach...?
Bird of prey	der Raubvogel	Straight on	Geradeaus
Wild cat	die Wildkatze	Left	Links
Wild boar	das Wildschwein/	Right	Rechts
	das Schwarzwild		
Moufflon	der Muffel/das	**Accommodation**	
	Mufflewild	Rooms	Zimmer
Roe deer	das Reh	Rooms to let,	
Red deer	das Rotwild	vacancies	Zimmer frei
Stag	der Hirsch	Bed	das Bett
Fox	der Fuchs	Shower	die Dusche
Fungi/		Bath	das Bad
mushrooms	die Pilzen	Key	der Schlußel
Lichen	die Flechte	Breakfast	das Frühstück
Owl	die Eule/der Uhu	Lunch	das Mittagessen
Capercaille	der Auerhahn	Dinner (pm)	das Abendessen
		Evening meal	
Reservoir	die Talsperre/der	(uncooked)	das Abendrot
	Stausee	Toilets	die Toiletten, das
Mine	das Bergwerk		Klo
Silver	das Silber	Ladies	Damen
Waterwheel	das Wasserrad	Gentlemen	Herren
Rocks and Tors	die Klippen	Vacant	Frei
Summit	der Gipfel	Occupied	Besetzt
Pond	der Teich	Lift	der Fahrstuhl
		Telephone	das Telefon
Please ...	Bitte	To telephone	Anrufen
Thank you	Danke schön		
Excuse me ...	Entschuldigen Sie	I have reserved	Ich habe ein
	bitte...	a room	Zimmer reserviert

What time is breakfast?	Um wieviel Uhr wird das Früstück serviert?
Breakfast is from...to...	Das Frühstück ist von... bis...
What time is it?	Wie spät ist es?
Is this seat/place free?	Bitte, ist der Platz/ Sitz frei?
No, it's taken	Nein, der Platz ist reserviert
Yes, it's free	Ja, bitte sehr

Food and Drink

Meal	das Essen
Menu	die Karte
Soup	die Suppe
Venison goulash	Hirsch/ Rehgoulasch
Roast boar	Wildschweinbraten
Pork (roast)	Schweinsbraten
Trout	die Forelle
Fish	der Fisch
Fruit	das Obst
Bread	das Brot
Bread roll	das Brötchen
Boiled egg	gekochtes Ei
Egg (fried/ scrambled)	das Spiegelei/ die Rühreier
Potatoes	die Kartoffel
Boiled potatoes with parsley	Petersilienkartoffel
Cabbage (green)	Kraut
Cabbage (red)	Rotkohl/Rotkraut
Kale	Grünkohl
Peas	die Erbsen
Beans (green)	die grüne Bohnen
Asparagus	der Spargel
Spinach	der Spinat

Apple juice with mineral water	Apfelschorle
Milk	die Milch
Cheese	der Käse

Ice cream	das Eis
Beer	das Bier
(though usually asked for by brand name or eiz Pils)	
Tea	der Tee
Coffee	der Kaffee
Water	das Wasser
Mineral water	das Mineralwasser
Apple (grape, orange) juice	Apfel (Trauben/ Orangen/Apfel- sinnen) saft
Wine	der Wein
Cream	die Sahne
With cream	mit Sahne
Without cream	ohne Sahne
Butter	die Butter
Sugar	der Zucker
Jam	die Konfiture/die Marmalade
Honey	der Honig
Salt	das Salz
Pepper	der Pfeffer

Bilberries	die Heidelbeeren
Strawberries	die Erdbeeren
Raspberries	die Himbeeren
Cake	der Kuchen
Gâteau	die Torte
Chocolate	die Schokolade
Cake and pastry shop	die Konditorei

Did you enjoy your meal?	Hat Ihnen das Essen geschmeckt? *or* Hat's geschmeckt? (colloquial)
Yes, very much	Ja, sehr
The bill	Bitte Zahlen/die Rechnung

Transport

Single	Einfach
Return	Hin-und-Zurück

Luggage	das Gepäck	Ambulance	der Krankenwagen
Platform	der Bahnstieg, das Gleis (bay)	Accident	der Unfall
		Insurance	die Versicherung
To change trains	Umsteigen	Police	die Polizei
No smoking	Nicht rauchen	Help!	Hilfe!
Timetable	der Fahrplan	Lost	Verloren
Departures	Abfahrt	Stolen	Gestohlen
Arrivals	Ankunft	I have a toothache	Ich habe Zahnweh
		Hayfever	der Heuschnupfen
What is the fare to...?	Wieviel kostet es nach...?	A cold	der Schnupfen
		Headache	die Kopfschmerzen
From which platform does it leave?	Von welchen Bahnsteig fährt er?	Stomach ache	die Magen-schmerzen
		Heart attack	der Herzanfall
		Diabetes	die Zucker-krankheit, die Diabetes
Narrow gauge railway	die Schmalspurbahn		
Steam engine	der Dampflok	Allergy	die Allergie
Airport	der Flughafen	Sunburn	der Sonnenbrand
Bus stop	die Autobus	Sickness, nausea	die Übelkeit
Haltestelle		Blister	die Blase
One-way street	Einbahnstraße	A sprained (ankle, knee)	(der Knöchel, das Knie) verstauchen
Taxi	das Taxi		
Petrol	das Benzin	Elastoplast, sticking plaster	das Pflaster
Diesel (oil)	der Diesel		
Bike	das Fahrrad	Chemist's shop	die Apotheke

General

Tourist inform-ation office	das Fremden-verkehrsamt
Post office	das Postamt
Bank	die Sparkasse
Passport	der Reisepaß
Currency chang-ing	Geldwechsel
Travellers cheques	die Reisechecks

*   *   *

Doctor	der Artz
Dentist	der Zahnartz
Pain	der Schmerz
Hospital	das Krankenhaus
Nurse	die Kranken-schwester

FURTHER READING

There is very little up-to-date reading matter about the whole of the Harz area in English, since after World War II till 1990 the Harz was divided between East and West Germany under two different regimes, travel was restricted, maps often deliberately inaccurate and information about East Germany generally was difficult to obtain. *The Green Guide to Germany* by Fleur and Colin Speakman, published by Greenprint, Merlin Press, remedies this to some extent and has an up-to-date section on the Harz. Even in Germany, till very recently, it was also impossible to obtain a reliable guide to the whole region.

The situation is now changing rapidly and a wealth of maps, leaflets and guidebooks of all kinds are starting to appear. If your German is fluent, an excellent modern guide is *Der Reisebegleiter Der Harz* by Rolf Schneider, published by Argon Verlag, which is also extremely well illustrated, with maps of the key towns and a useful overall map of the Harz. The *Bild Atlas* on the Harz deals solely with the western Harz, but is of the usual good standard and will probably be revised to take in the east in due course.

Particularly recommended for the rail enthusiast is the fully illustrated guide in English and German entitled *Mit Volldampf auf den Brocken* by Volker Schadach and Friedrich Menge, published by Studio Volker Shaddach, Goslar. *Auf dem Brocken* by Dr Hartmut Knappe, published by the Harzmuseum Wenigerode, is a very useful guide to all the different aspects of the Brocken with contributions by other experts and Gerhard Eckert's *Der Brocken - Berg in Deutschland*, published by Husum, provides further extensive information. For readers particularly interested in mining industrial archaeology, there are detailed publications by the Rammelsberg mine, for example, which are of a high standard.

Printed by CARNMOR PRINT & DESIGN,
95-97 LONDON ROAD, PRESTON, LANCASHIRE, UK.

144